A UNIVERSE APART

Against the Tide

John Cockerill

Kingdom Publishers

A Universe Apart
Against the Tide
Copyright© John Cockerill

All rights reserved. No part of this book may be reproduced in any form by photocopying or any electronic or mechanical means, including information storage or retrieval systems, without permission in writing from both the copyright owner and the publisher of the book. The right of John Cockerill to be identified as the author of this work has been asserted by him in accordance with the Copyright, Designs and Patents Act 1988 and any subsequent amendments thereto.
A catalogue record for this book is available from the British Library.

All Scripture Quotations have been taken from the New International Version and the King James Version of the Bible.

ISBN: 978-1-913247-63-8

1st Edition by Kingdom Publishers
Kingdom Publishers
London, UK.
You can purchase copies of this book from any leading bookstore or email **contact@kingdompublishers.co.uk**

I wish to dedicate this book to my late wife Caroline, together we endured that dreadful familiar spirit experience, and out of it found Jesus together.

ACKNOWLEDGMENTS

A big thank you to Jon Tiley, my computer guru, where without his help this book would still be languishing in the bowels of my PC.

Throughout the pandemic, Helen and Stuart Walters provided for all my need's, allowing me to isolate and proceed with these writings, so very much appreciated.

Permission obtained from Mark Williams, Managing Director, Day One, Rylands Road, Leominster, HR6 8NZ, by e-mail on 17/9/2020, to use text from "Hallmarks of design by Stuart Burgess."

Professor Burgess article on the "eye" of the Peacock is a real eye opener, as he further expands its complexities in greater depth.

Unwise men of old though you may not believe it,
Considered creation and how they conceive it,

That all living things whatever they be,
Just emerged and became everything you can see,
It's called evolution or pre self-design.
Derived through a process of chance and of time,
A muddled confusion,
of faith and delusion,
And error of science that borders on crime.

The atheists tool for the elimination
Of God for all time from creations equation.

CONTENTS

FOREWORD	13
PROLOGUE	15
INTRODUCTION	17
CHAPTER ONE	19
Optimal not Optional	19
The Rear Gunner	20
Puzzling Pollination	21
Nearer Home	22
Design for Purpose	24
An Eye for Colour	25
CHAPTER TWO	27
Our Universal Home	27
Top of the List	29
CHAPTER THREE	33
In the Beginning	33
CHAPTER FOUR	37
Can these Bones Live?	37
Restoration	41
Prime Movers	43
CHAPTER FIVE	50
I Am Written in the Scrolls	50
CHAPTER SIX	60
Not a Species	60
CHAPTER SEVEN	71
This King was a Head of Gold	71

CHAPTER EIGHT	77
Fifty-two Days	77
CHAPTER NINE	91
So Who? The Devil, is it?	91
CHAPTER TEN	100
Pear-shaped in a Garden	100
CHAPTER ELEVEN	106
The Ultimate Crucible	106
CHAPTER TWELVE	115
A very Desirable Inheritance	115
CONCLUSION	118

FOREWORD

There are some who would say that a person with experience is never at the mercy of a person with an argument. Sadly, in recent days, this has been an excuse for many Christians to ditch using their brains and intellectual faculties and resort to dependence upon heart-warming experiences to evaluate the fundamentals and bedrock of faith. Of course, there has to be a balance, but of late, the pendulum does seem to have swung more frequently into the arena of subjective expression rather than an erudite examination of evidence and history.

John Cockerill bucks the trend. By his own admission, he is not in the flush of youth but his years have provided him with the opportunity to turn from an atheistic position to a strong stance on his Christian beliefs – accrued by using his extraordinary intellectual examination of Biblical history and prophecy, and his God given powers of apologetic reasoning and thought.

Yet this journey was enhanced, and some would say encouraged, by a subjective experience that occupied the minds of his wife Carol and himself in the late Sixties. I was privileged to be on the periphery of that journey, as the persons who prompted John and Carol's understanding of the deception and confusion happened to be close friends of mine. John's horrific account is factual and true, and his testimony is rightly placed in the middle of his deliberations, providing the fulcrum whereby the weight of his propositions are substantiated.

Who was it who said that the devil always overplays his hand? For John, this evil encounter prompted research into the validity of the Christian faith, as he sought to answer the many age old questions that antagonists have conjured up down through the centuries. His findings are the endorsement of his conclusions.

This book provides an insight into what happens when the head and the heart combine to evaluate the essence of Christian Truth. Although many have written on the theme of 'intelligent design', fulfilment of prophecy and the redundancy of modern culture, John's insights are unique through the application of his own experience and journey of faith.

A welcome addition to the current growth of well researched documentation that adds increasing weight to the role and relevance of Christian values in 21st Century society.

Dave Pope
CEO: Flame Trust.
January 2021.

PROLOGUE

Almost from the time that I moved from atheism to Christianity, I developed an appetite for the creation versus evolution question. I am no academic, I earned my crusts as a refrigeration engineer, now retired, and at eighty four years of age, the interest has not waned.

Our education systems are now heavily weighted towards the teaching that all things evolved, so, inevitably scientists grounded in its culture attribute their professional findings to that model. Several expanding concerns compelled me to re-visit my many notes, gleaned from multifarious sources over the years, and then to attempt to mould them into a coherent form in order to address those issues. This book is the product of that re-visiting.

I have a concern, for those Christians who in education absorbed those theories, and now struggle to reconcile their faith with its claims. I have a concern, for those now in education both young and older, being fed daily its erroneous doctrine. I have a concern, that despite their 100% proven accuracy, biblical Scripture is dismissed out of hand, replaced by fanciful conjecture.

A few examples of scriptural fore-telling are included as evidence.

Logic and common sense are available to us all, and I have endeavoured to employ them, together with simplicity and brevity. In depth scientific understanding in order to defend biblical creation, is only, in many cases, needed, because pre-programmed mindsets are continually weaving evolution into authentic discoveries, thus needlessly expanding its complexities.

My ultimate hope in writing this book is that many who read it, will reconsider their opinion on the origin of all things, placing the credit where it rightfully belongs, with our amazing God.

INTRODUCTION

During the late 19th century, a new religion was born; it claimed to have found the answers to all our questions relating to the origin of life, thereby rendering all other considerations as inconsequential throwbacks to a bygone age.

Unfortunately, science with its indisputable benefits to mankind in multifarious ways has been hijacked by atheists enthusiastically embracing its undeniable potential to further their cause.

The dominance of evolutionary thinking prevails throughout the whole spectrum of society; in education, government, life style and attitude, its theories are now made law, being the lawful model permitted to be taught in our education establishments. The effect of this philosophy of live for today because that is all there is, is very obvious. We are given through this faith, a mandate to behave in any way we please, and if that way be anti-social or positively immoral, so what? Our portion is to live briefly, die inevitably, then be as if we had never been, how sad. yet so effective is the evangelical campaigning of its media spokes-persons that we unquestioningly accept their statements, having total faith in their credibility.

The acceptance that all things came together by chance is now inevitable for several generations. Children are told that evolution rules OK, so it is understandable that as many move on into the sciences, this will be the model within which they will work, and the possibility of a conflicting concept is not even contemplated. Statements unproved pepper the dialogues in most nature documentaries.

The porcupine evolved those spikes for his protection - how?
This male bird developed these colors to attract females - how?
This is an amazing development in its evolution progress.

All trotted out as facts without a shred of cast iron evidence to support them except the many miraculous millions of years and countless fortuitous mutations.

Unless otherwise specified, all Bible quotations are taken from The New International Version Bible (NIV), Copyright © 1973 1978 1984 2011 by Biblica, Inc.™

CHAPTER ONE
Optimal not Optional

Let us begin to question evolutionary thinking by dipping into some of the ubiquitous instances of optimum design, where all components essentially come together in perfection at the same time.

Anything continuously in a state of transition, is not of an optimum design. For instance, most man-made things are constantly being modified in order to improve efficiency. Only in creation is true optimum design to be found, the reason being that nothing living could exist in a transitory condition. There are no transitional forms to be found on Earth, living or fossilised, everything had to be designed to live and function perfectly within its designated purpose,

Science and the Creation account given in Genesis are in agreement that the first living things on our planet were plants. With evolution they began first of all in the sea, then made their way on to land, in Genesis they all came together at the same time. Nevertheless, that which was needed from the outset in both cases was the ability to photosynthesise. As we look into this it is important to keep in mind that at this point nothing existed Prior to plants there would have been nothing to eat. In the light of their importance, it is incredible that the very first things to inhabit our Earth had programmed within them so complex and sophisticated a facility.

Photosynthesis is known as a life-harvesting. Complex, chlorophyl is the molecule that absorbs sunlight; each one only five thousandths of a millimeter in diameter, yet they carry out what must surely be (with pollination) the most vital life-perpetuating work on the planet. These molecules take two photons of sunlight and, using electromagnetic energy, split water molecules into their individual elements of hydrogen and oxygen, the oxygen is then ejected as waste and the hydrogen utilised for the plants needs. This is a very brief outline; the whole system is extremely sophisticated.

How could such a complex system as this have come about by chance? The mechanism on which all subsequent life on Earth would be dependent, and common to all vegetation from the beginning. Out of absolute necessity it would have to come together as of optimum design; a system akin to a national lottery could not have formed it.

The Rear Gunner

Consider the dangerous systems that endowed the bombardier beetle with his amazing defense equipment. Two chemicals, hydroquinone and hydrogen peroxide, are stored together in two specially constructed chambers, there is no reaction and they are always ready for use, leading from those compartments are two combustion tubes, when the beetle is threatened, he squeezes a charge of this solution into those tubes, there an enzyme, is released, which catalyses the rapid decomposition of hydrogen peroxide into oxygen and water, another enzyme, peroxidase, catalyses the oxidation of the hydroquinones. This raises the liquid in the combustion chambers to the boiling point of water and the excess oxygen creates a high pressure.

A valve in the entrance to the combustion chamber closes to prevent this pressure from affecting his internal organs, and the chambers themselves are so constructed that they will not rupture, at the desired moment a valve in the chamber opens, with a pop the scalding liquid is directed accurately at his potential killer through two directional turrets at his rear. Some African *bombardiers* can swivel their turrets through 270 degrees. He is able to sustain his firing up to 20 times at 22mph.

A step-by-step development is inconceivable due to the inevitability of self destruction during the formation. Our beetle poses numerous questions, none more puzzling than, how did he know which enzymes to utilise to catalyze his chemicals to achieve his desired reactions? Then, how would he learn how to store them safely within his body? One tiny error, during his experimental stage would have been disastrous. Furthermore is the necessity to reprogram his DNA to perpetuate his invention. If there were but one example of optimum design of a living entity on Earth, it should need investigation, but they are incalculable. It is obvious that this little insect had to have come together instantaneously. You may be thinking, hold on that would need to be a work of creation: yes, it would.

Puzzling Pollination

Our natural world is so familiar to us that we simply accept all at face value. We need to pause and really observe beyond form and function, taking that which we have been informed of by honest scientific investigation, looking beyond the given facts and asking the question, how?

For example, some instances of pollination symbiosis are so clever they defy logical explanation. We see, read or hear of them, marvel briefly at them, then move on. In its season the mirror orchid, *orphreys speculum*, ensures its pollination. The small bee that distributes its pollen emerges and promptly sets off in search of a mate. Sadly, for him, his potential mate's life cycle is so designed that she will not be around for a month. However, this crafty plant has formed in its flower, the perfect image of the female bee our male is seeking. Thinking he has found her, he hones in on the imposter; disappointed, he flies away laden with pollen to distribute among the other deceivers.

Some orchids are even more remarkable in their deceptive ploys. As if visual imitations were not enough, some can produce fake pheromones making them irresistible to male pollinators. In fact so realistic is the deception that sperm has been found on flowers. When you consider the practical realities involved here, questions arise that deserve answers. If plants can produce scents to attract pollinators, by what process do they recognise the smell they wish to replicate? Do some plants possess a sense of smell? How do they translate that aroma into a biological chemical production facility within themselves?

How are these plants able to observe the female bee it wants to copy, and then are able to produce an exact image in its own flower? The *Angaecum Sesquipedale* is a plant that has a nectar tube 12" long. When Charles Darwin observed it he said there must be a moth with a probiscis long enough to reach the nectar, sure enough, in 1903 the *xanthopan morgani moth* was discovered. It has a proboscis 12" long and has since been photographed feeding at night on this very plant.

If they were not formed at the same time, how did one exist without the other? Evolutions answer, as I understand it, is co-evolution; as one grew so grew the other to match it, a bit of a chicken and egg type puzzle.

Nearer Home

Our human brain is considered to be the most sophisticated thing in the universe. So before we have a simple look at it, consider this: on an Earth clock of 24 hours, humans arrived on the planet in our present form around a few seconds to midnight. By that time, most other living things would, according to evolution, have achieved their desired form. So how is it that man, with his incredible brain, arrived so far advanced? The leap from ape simplicity to human sophistication is unbelievable, but more of that later.

Our brain weighs in at around 1.5 kilograms and consists of one hundred billion nerve cells, it is the center of our nervous system, and takes twenty years to mature, passing information up to one thousand trillion times. In the womb it grows at a rate of eight thousand cells per second; we are made up of around one hundred and twenty trillion cells. Those cells needed for balance and coordination are equal to all the rest put together. The reason for including this is that as we ponder the enormity of our complexity, it is worth considering the improbability of it all coming together by chance.

A late eminent evolutionary scientist has stated, "I regard the brain as a computer which will stop working when its components fail, there is no heaven or after life for broken down computers, that is a fairy story for those afraid of the dark."

In spite of his unquestionable intelligence, it appears that he had not computed into his equations the consideration that today's computers are an ever-improving product of enormous amounts of research, meticulous long considered designs by teams of highly qualified gifted individuals in several countries. The bottom line is that this scientist together with many others, thinks this awesome complex human brain is the product of a mindless lottery that designed itself, proving if nothing else that there is a definable difference between intelligence and wisdom.

Our amazing brain can store memories long forgotten, that can come flooding back should we encounter a stimulant such as a smell, a sound, a piece of music or a voice. Even a taste can unexpectedly transport us back in time as if it were yesterday. This rapid memory facility also acts as a self-preservation device as our senses assess whatever we have encountered, and advise us to either relax or take evasive action.

Our perception of reality is framed by our sight, as our brains through a process called visual perception, make adjustments that enable us to comprehend distances, shapes, angles etc. In fact our eyes could not work at all without every necessary component, including the brains interpretations of the eyes observations being present at the time our whole systems were formed: yet another case of optimum design.

To ascribe the perfection of intricate complexities, perfection of design, essential inter-dependencies, together with ubiquitous instances of optimum design as the products of haphazard chance and fortuitous multiple mutations, requires a very special sort of faith, and for too long now this religion of no hope has held sway through its pseudo-scientific theories.

Design for Purpose

It really can lift your spirit on a warm summer day to see the bumble bee working away among the flowers, each one fully equipped for the task he has to carry out. He reminds me of a tradesman, a carpenter or an electrician, as he sets off for work wearing that leather belt containing the tools of his trade: easily accessible.

Likewise, when our little bumble sets off on his days' work, he too is perfectly equipped for his job. His two back legs have wonderfully designed baskets or pouches into which he can safely store his collection, his two middle legs have a thorn like probe for extracting pollen from its *basket*. On each of his front legs he has a comb which he uses to clean the hairs on his head and antenna. On his back legs, he also has rows of stiff hairs used to brush the pollen off his body into the *basket*. On his other side, his tongue is long enough to reach the nectar in most plants whilst allowing his hairy body to make contact with the pollen, and so allowing him to carry out his most valuable work: pollination. The bee is indeed a masterpiece of design.

Meanwhile, back in the hive, the bees shape their cells with perfect mathematical accuracy, attaining maximum strength with greatest capacity while using the least amount of wax. Outside the hive, the other bees are dancing their clever communication, indicating direction, distance and wind strength to their found food source. In this one little creature we see the epitome of efficiency.

An Eye for Colour

Most of us are familiar with the *eye pattern* on the tail feathers of the peacock; what process do they have in common with the colours produced by a petrol spillage on wet tarmac? The answer is that they are both products of the same effect known as *thin film interference,* so called because of its interference with the wavelengths of white light, that produce colors in certain circumstances.

The agent at work on the tarmac is oil or petrol, the colours being dependent on the thickness of each layer, the background of necessity being dark. The agent at work on the peacock's *eye* is keratin, found widely and used in nature, our hair, nails, in some insects and animal horns, and much more, In the *eye* the keratin is in layers of three, the thickness of each layer being crucial to the production of the correct colour and its position in the display. A micron is $1{,}000^{th}$ of a millimeter and each layer is only 0.03 to 1.5 microns thick. The colours in the feature are, dark purple in the center with a blue surround; then a larger area of bronze with a green area blending into a darker green, the only pigment is in the dark background.

To have achieved its desired design, the primitive emerging bird would, first of all need to be aware of the pattern it wanted, a sort of pre-conceived design. It would need to have an understanding of white light and how keratin could be used to create thin film interference, together with knowledge of how to work this into its metabolism and through its Peacock DNA pass the information to future generations.

I know this is a ridiculous concept, but it is the bottom line: to cast away any involvement by an intelligent creator we are left with a mental picture of primitive creatures having no knowledge of the sciences yet able to achieve within themselves the most complex innovations that we with our vast resources, are unable to produce.

To speak in terms of a creature's development as if it had any control over it, is crazy, either you recognise the hand of a creator or the concept of an abandonment to the lottery of chance, fortuitous mutations. These are the only two proposals on the table at present.

Charles Darwin once said, "The sight of a feather in a peacock's tail whenever I gaze at it, makes me feel sick" It does not equate with evolutionist thinking.

CHAPTER TWO
Our Universal Home

Our understanding of our planet, Earth, is that it is spectacularly unique. Every moment of every day someone somewhere on it is scanning way out into space, looking to increase our portfolio of understanding of it, always seeking for other worlds that may support life.

Come fly with me , and in your imagination rise far above earth's atmosphere, to view our universal home, shining like a jewel set in a black velvet infinity, to marvel at its pristine sensitivity, its isolation, diametrically separated from its dead and dying neighbours.

Have you ever considered our vulnerability in the vastness of space?

Light travels at 670,616,629, miles per hour, or 5.88 trillion miles per year, so, a light year is 5.88 trillion miles. Our *milky way* galaxy is 100,000 light years across. The largest galaxy cluster yet found is 1c1101, the Abel cluster, and is six million light years in diameter and 1.7 billion light years from our sun, it is estimated that there are at least 350 billion galaxies in the known universe, and in Earth travel terms, Voyager Two in 2020 was within 2.5 trillion miles of Sirius.

Set all this against Earth's 7,937 mile diameter, yes miles (food for thought), and you will grasp something of our *apparent* insignificance. We are travelling at 66,660 miles per hour around an enormous nuclear powerhouse that constantly pours out a lethal cocktail of hydrogen, helium, high energy particles, gamma rays, ultra violet light, x rays and protons, which by the time they reach Earth, are traveling at one million miles per hour; solar winds that could wipe out all life on Earth in an instant. Our journey is through an intensely cold, black, endless vacuum where there is no up nor down, no air to breath or sustenance of any kind, just an empty void, and here we are speeding through it, filled with life and exceedingly verdant. So why, out of all the numerous cosmic spheres investigated, is our Earth so spectacularly unique?

The case is well documented and communicated. It is considered that all matter was formed from particle interaction, possibly on a quantum scale. Genesis states that *in the beginning the Earth was without form and void* so, no disparity there. But the big question will not go away, why is our Earth so vastly different?

For the same reason that it is filled with such made for purpose diverse life forms, it was designed to be a perfect habitation for every living thing on it. It did not just happen; it was created. Let me explain why I believe this in ways familiar to us all.

Everything speaks of a designer who from the very outset had in mind the comfort and protection of those he made to inhabit Earth. We considered the hostile solar winds constantly bombarding us, yet despite our perilous surroundings, we are safe beneath our protective atmosphere. This canopy of ingenious layers is specifically designed for purpose, the protection and preservation of all life on Earth. It burns up around five hundred meteorites a day, absorbs harmful radiation, warms Earth's surface and reduces extremes of temperatures between day and night. Our atmosphere is itself protected by our magnetic field, our first line of defense that deflects away those solar winds. We can witness this happening when we view the northern lights.

Our seasons, so vital for food growth, have been provided for by Earths 23.4 degree tilt. Any significant deviation would seriously affect both our seasons and weather patterns. Earth rotates at 1,000 miles an hour, giving us our day and night, so providing order in our lives. One revolution around the sun takes 365 days 23 hours and 56 minutes; this is one gigantic chronometer.

We are never left in total darkness; we have a light for the day and one for the night. The moon is on average 250 thousand miles away, any significant difference would result in tidal surges on a twice-a-day basis. Metals, coal and all manner of minerals are simply waiting to be found and utilised for our good. Herbs and fruits reproduce themselves year on year in so many varieties. There are plants with medicinal properties, many found and more no doubt waiting to be discovered, fertile soils containing all the nutrients plants require and scenery to gladden our hearts, or to enjoy, climbing, swimming, walking whatever.

All vegetation is predominantly green, the most restful colour for our eyes. We jump on planes to be under the blue sky, can you imagine the sky being any other than blue? A self- regulating weather system, that is until we interfered with it. There are trees of many varieties each offering different properties in their timber for our use, and, of course, our brain that has taught us how to utilise all these provisions.

Top of the List

When providing for all life on Farth, undoubtedly water would have been top of the list, there can be no life without it. Take two highly reactive hydrogen atoms each with its one electron, and unite it with one equally volatile oxygen atom with its six electrons (is far happier with eight). The oxygen orbits are filled, their mutual volatilities cease and we have that incredible fire–quenching, life-sustaining, universal solvent we take so much for granted.

It is only as we consider the properties of this wonderful compound that we realise how special it really is. It has qualities like no other. Its specific heat is higher than most other compounds so that anything that retains it, including our bodies, will be slow to heat and slow to cool, and so maintains a regular, more comfortable temperature. The vast oceans are thus able to retain their constant temperatures ensuring the well-being of all that inhabit them.

Yet another of its life preserving properties is encountered as temperatures drop. Most liquids become denser as they cool down and continue to do so until they reach freezing point, not so with water. At four degrees centigrade an astonishing thing happens. As with most other liquids its density increases until that four-degree cut off point is reached, but then in water the process is reversed with its density decreasing and continuing to do so, until freezing point, zero degrees centigrade where it turns to ice. Now being less dense than the liquid water from which it was formed, it floats, and so provides a protective barrier from the extreme cold above, and a warmer environment for the abundant life that inhabit those arctic waters below.

The placing of Earth within our solar system is no accident. Its exact location is critical. Venus is too near the Sun and Mars too far away to support water. We orbit between the two and are perfectly situated to accommodate this life-sustaining liquid in all its forms, water, ice, vapour. In the creator's infinite wisdom, no aspect of our total environment has been overlooked.

My ears pricked up when I heard a professor on TV in an excellent documentary on gravity, having been spun in a gravity inducing machine, say, "we are tuned to live on a planet that has only 1 G". It was the word *tuned* that drew my attention, it is a word that speaks of the involvement of a contemplated requirement.

Every planet and moon discovered is scanned for evidence of water; past or present. There is no shortage of it in the universe, but what we seek is water held in its liquid form, capable of supporting life: the search for extra terrestrial life continues daily. In fact, the need to find another orb that could support human habitation has gone up a few notches since the growing awareness of the vulnerability of our own planet.

Such a potential inter-planetary evacuation will not take place; there is no *planet B*. Mars is the strongest contender, there is surface evidence of the possibility of water beneath it, but what of the violent dust storms, the extreme temperatures or the prospect of living in an artificial world with a total lack of natural oxygen? Moreover, how many of us seven billion would be able to escape? Would you want to live there?

Any destination outside of our immediate solar system is out of the question because of the immense distances involved. Even should a suitable place be found, it could take a lifetime or more to travel there. Finally, consider procreation in a weightless environment. Although it may be an interesting and fun logistical exercise, would it, as seen in experiments carried out on animals, not be loaded and doomed with biological problems.

This Earth was created by God as a home for all He made to live on it; we will never find another like it. He formed it for a purpose (which we look at later) and there is no need for another. Before we leave these thoughts of mankind's fear for the future and his need to consider the provision of a place of escape, the whole of Earth's story, past present and future, is written in the Bible, and yes, the Earth and the heavens will one day, as the Scriptures say, *be rolled up like a scroll*, (Isaiah 34:4) and there will be a new Heaven and a new Earth. In this fact alone we recognise the hope of those that believe in God and the hopelessness of those who have made evolution their *god*.

CHAPTER THREE
In the Beginning

The first words of Scripture state, *in the beginning God*, telling that He is, followed by *created the heavens and the Earth*. (Genesis 1:1) No man existed, he had not yet been formed, therefore, all information relating to events at that time would have to be communicated to someone, and that person was Moses, who wrote the book of Genesis.

It would have been impossible in that day and age to pass on the complete history of the very early age of Earth, but the scant details we are given contain sufficient information for us to build up a picture of its early history. The first clue yielding passage, is Genesis 1:6-8, *And God said, "let there be an expanse between the waters to separate water from Water" so God made the expanse and separated the water under the expanse from the water above it and it was so. God called the expanse, sky.*

We see that there were *waters* on the Earth, and above the Earth, above the firmament, our atmosphere. It seems that the Earth was completely surrounded by waters, no doubt held as are our clouds in vapour form. The second relevant Scripture is Genesis 2:5-6, *...for the Lord had not caused it to rain upon the Earth. but a mist came up from the Earth, and watered the whole surface of the ground*. It may not seem much to go on, but based on what we have been given, we see a completely different Earth to the one we now inhabit.

There was no rain, the Earth was watered by a mist, put that together with the water canopy enveloping the whole Earth and we see our planet, in its earliest times, bathed in constant temperature, a controlled greenhouse effect with the water canopy acting like glass. At the same time it would be further restricting those toxic solar winds so harmful to all life. The mist provided humidity, and increased oxygen pressure would have enabled longevity, and the whole environment would favour *giantism*, vegetation would have grown unrestricted, vast forests would have covered all lands.

A similar notion has recently been considered by evolutionists in order to explain in particular, the existence of giant flying insects, as in today's atmospheric pressure they would be unable to fly. The pressure would have been too high to support human life. Evolutionists, therefore, based those levels according to those insects needs; conjecture. The biblical account sits very comfortably into our understanding of the early Earth, but there is more.

We need to dip into the story of that much misunderstood character, Noah, to further this investigation. The flood of Noah, denied by evolutionists, was not just a major catastrophic event, nor was it an act of God brought about for no other reason than that He could, so He did. It was an event that mankind brought upon himself. Ever since Adam's disobedience in Eden the barometer of sin had been rising. Man, this companion God had made with whom to fellowship, was fast heading to self-destruction. Let us hear it from God's point of view.

In Genesis 6:5-8 we read, *the Lord saw how great man's wickedness on Earth had become, and that every inclination of the thoughts of his heart was only evil all the time. the Lord was grieved that he had made man on the Earth, and his heart was filled with pain. So, the Lord said, "I will wipe mankind whom I have created from the face of the Earth man and* animals, and creatures that move along the ground and birds of the air for I am grieved that I have made them".

⁸*But Noah found favour in the eyes of the Lord.*

So, God told Noah of His intention to drown the Earth, how? We do not know, it may have been in a dream, or a vision, a spoken conversation or through Noah's inner thoughts. It is well documented that God speaks to people today in many different ways.

God *told* Noah to build an ark, a floating vessel. No doubt Noah would have endured a great deal of ridicule during the years he was building it.

What on Earth are you doing Noah?

Water coming down from the sky? Don't talk rubbish!

God told you to do it? You are even more crazy than you look.

Similar no doubt to those encountered by Christians today as they tell of God's intentions for our present generations.

It is doubtful that many people have really considered the true nature of that flood. It was no gentle rain from heaven; forty days and nights of driving rain would have been catastrophic. You may have seen on TV, or have experienced for yourselves the effect of heavy rainfall: property damage, landslides etc. But this flood was something else, it was not just heavy rain. That vast store of water surrounding the planet collapsed, all the great fountains of the deep were broken up (there are water spouts beneath the sea today). At the first indication of the flood people would be hammering on the door of the ark, realising that for all of those years, Noah had been right, but he could not let them in, as Genesis 7:16 tells, *then the Lord shut him in.* (Christian, does that sound familiar?)

The power of uncontrolled water is incredible. The results of its destructive energy would have had effects beyond our wildest imagination with huge landslides and tsunamis of indescribable proportions. The forests that covered the ground would have been flattened and swept away by the raging waters, deposited in great piles in valleys and low- lying entrapment areas (future coal seams?). These in turn would have been covered by many meters or even miles of rock and other debris as the waters swirled relentlessly around the planet. We are told they covered the whole Earth, even the mountains were under water.

This situation continued for forty days and nights, and though the flooding had stopped, the waters remained for a further 150 days, but what of Noah and his valuable cargo? No doubt they would have had a rough ride, but survival was inevitable. God had shut them in, and he would have ensured their safety. Noah stepped out of the ark into a different world to the one he had known pre-flood. He would notice a marked difference in temperature between day and night, the sky, no longer hidden by vapourised water surrounding the Earth, was blue with white fluffy clouds, stars were now clearly visible, and the sun and moon gave brighter light.

The mist that had risen from the ground was no longer there, and it now rained to water his crops. Noah would not have been aware of it but some changes were not to his benefit. The removal of that water barrier now allowed more of those toxic solar winds to penetrate our Earth, which together with the decreased oxygen levels, reduced humidity and other factors, would henceforth contribute to the gradual decrease in life expectancy of all things.

Rapid evaporation produces rapid refrigeration, and the speed at which the flood had enabled this to happen, is evidenced in the many animals found frozen, perfectly preserved, still blissfully chewing on flowers as they froze to death, in what are now the coldest regions on Earth. Great changes had taken place, most evident in geology and geography, leaving us with the world now familiar to all.

Nothing in God's account of the early Earth is out of sync with any discovery made in it. I do believe in the almighty power of God, that in six days He is able to make the heavens and the Earth and all that is in them, I also know that a thousand years is as a day to Him; (2 Peter 3 He inhabits eternity, time itself did not exist until He created the universe, and, radio–metric dating is far from infallible as we shall consider later.

In John 9 we read how Jesus in a moment created sight in a man born without sight. There are some incredible prophesies contained in the Bible, and there is overwhelming evidence of God's communication with His people and the infallibility of His word, be it spoken or written. Nowhere on Earth is there a greater wealth of forecasted events becoming reality. Evidence not only that He is, but also that He never ceases to be involved in our lives.

CHAPTER FOUR
Can these Bones Live?

That the Jewish people should be known as *God's people* is an offence to many. The reason being that they are unaware of why. Since Adam, God has wanted a people that would live differently to other people on Earth, a people that would follow after Him and shine as beacons in this perpetually darkening moral world. He chose a man of faith, Abraham, and through his grandson, Jacob, whose name God changed to Israel, formed the nation of that name.

The detail of their history is too extensive to relate here, so for brevity we shall only touch on that which is relevant. You may be aware that the Jews were slaves in Egypt for four hundred years, and were brought together under the leadership of Moses. They then spent forty years in the wilderness as God formed them into His people.

Everything went well for a while, but gradually the people began to take part in the idolatrous practices of those cultures among which they lived, denying the God that had led them out of slavery in Egypt. They even sank so low as to sacrifice their own children to the wooden and stone gods of their neighbours.

God constantly sent prophets to remonstrate with them, some they stoned, some were imprisoned, and others they killed. God offered reconciliation if they did not follow after these false gods, but the Israelites would not listen. He warned them that if they continued living as they were, He would remove them from their land and scatter them to the four corners of the Earth. There are many Scriptures recording the warnings God gave to his people. I have just highlighted a few as examples of the graveness of their situation.

Way back in the book of Deuteronomy, while they were still wandering in the wilderness, Moses recorded this warning, *Just as it pleased the Lord to make you prosper and increase in number so it will please him to ruin and destroy you, you will be uprooted from the land you are entering to possess, then the Lord will scatter you through all nations from one end of the Earth to the other.* (Deuteronomy 28:63-64) The chapter continues by describing the life they would endure within those countries.

Dated about the same period, 1490BC, Leviticus continues with the same theme. *I will scatter you among the nations and I will draw out my sword and pursue you, your land will lay waste and your cities will lie in ruin.* (Leviticus 26:33) if you know anything about the land of Israel, you will recognise the truth of the prophesies written three thousand four hundred and sixty years ago.

It is necessary at this point to establish that it would have been impossible to add anything to the Jewish scrolls at a later date, for the following reasons. The books of the Old Testament, telling the Jewish history, date back thousands of years. They were translated in the third century before Christ by seventy two Jewish scholars working in Alexandria, to provide a copy for the famous library there, and the many Greek speaking Jews. This translation is called the Septuagint. Nothing has, or ever can be added to these documents, the strict oversight of the Jewish priesthood renders this impossible; the authenticity of those writings is absolute.

There are many more Scriptures that tell of the Lord's threat of expulsion from the land He had given to the Israelites, but in total disregard of these, the immoral life-styles the Israelites lived became worse and worse until it is recorded in 2 Chronicles 36:15-16 , it seems the Lord is saying enough is enough, and so we read these sad words. *The Lord God of their fathers sent word to them through his messengers again and again because he had pity on his people, and on his dwelling place, but they mocked Gods messengers despised his word and scoffed at his prophets until the wrath of the Lord was aroused against his people, and there was no remedy.* The eventual outcome of this was the expulsion from their land.

I include this section as it has prophetic relevance later. However, their eviction was not immediate; Israel split into two nations after the death of Solomon. Ten northern tribes, then known as Israel, and two southern tribes known as Judah. Israel was cast out first by the Assyrians. The eviction of Judah was in two parts; the first was by the hand of Nebuchadnezzar of Babylon, and the second and final one was carried out by the Romans under General Titus. Inevitably the land they had inhabited was left totally unattended and became wilderness, swamp and scrubland, exactly as the prophesy in Leviticus predicted.

Around 629BC, the prophet Jeremiah wrote, *their land will be waste an object of lasting scorn, all who pass by will be appalled and will shake their heads, like a wind from the east I will scatter them before their enemies, I will show them my back and not my face in the day of their disaster* (Jeremiah 18:16-17) This is exactly as history confirms it played out.

Pause a while and consider this, a nation banished from its land 2,500 years ago, scattered like snowflakes into the four corners of the Earth, absorbed into the life of many different nations, yet still retaining their national identity, for all that time observing the religious customs handed down through many generations. Each Jew would speak the language of their adopted country, and would be assimilated into that way of life, yet at a point written into both history and prophesy, occupied by you and I, they have been incredibly returned to the land of their fathers.

Even as I write, many Jews are returning to Israel, despite the probable hardships they are aware they may encounter, but in so doing, bringing about the desire of their hearts. All those centuries away from their homeland, every year at the feast of Passover the Jews quote the words, *next year in Jerusalem.*

Many think that God has washed His hands of His people, believing the Church to be the new Israel. However, in light of many references to His continued love, and future plans for them, that opinion holds no water.

Restoration

How could God possibly bring about the return of the whole nation of Israel after 2,500 years? And what means could He employ to achieve this? To move a people out of their land is the easier part physically, but how after so long would God be able to fulfill his promise to return them again to their own land? The prophet Ezekiel wrote, *I dispersed them among the nations, and they were scattered through the countries, I judged them according to their conduct and their actions"* he then goes on to say that which he was going to do would not be for their sake, *"but for My holy name which they have profaned.* (Ezekiel 36:19) and vs24 *for I will take you out of the nations, I will gather you back into your own land.*

The words of Isaiah in 712BC are of reconciliation and caring; God assuring His people that whatever befalls them He is always with them. Isaiah 43:5-6 he writes, *Do not be afraid for I am with you, I will bring your children from the east and gather you from the west, I will say to the north, give up, and to the south do not hold them back, bring my sons from afar and my daughters from the ends of the Earth.*

Ezekiel was taken by God to a valley of dry bones, carried we are told, by the spirit of the Lord, this valley was full of dry bones and God said to him, *can these bones live?* God then tells Ezekiel to prophesy over the bones. The bones came together with bone, then the tendons, then flesh, then skin, though at that point there was no breath in them, that comes later; you can find the story in Ezekiel 37.

Vs 11 sums it all up when God says to the prophet, "*son of man these bones are the whole house of Israel; they say our bones are dried up our hope is gone, we are cut off*", God then told him he was going to open up their graves and bring them up out of them."

The graves God speaks of here are the lands in which the Israelites are living. I feel a need to quote more from this chapter as its verses say it very clearly.

Therefore, prophesy and say to them: this is what the sovereign Lord says: O my People, I am going to open your graves and bring you up from them; I will Bring you back into the land of Israel, then you my people will know that I am the Lord, when I open your graves and bring you up from them. I will put my spirit in you and you will live, and I will settle you in your own land then you will know that I the Lord have spoken, and I have done it, declares the Lord". (Ezekiel 37:12-14-)

Prior to the earlier part of the 20th century, the probability of the Jews returning to their own land was unthinkable, yet now anyone born after 1948 has known no world other than the one in which the nation of Israel exists. These incredibly accurate forecasts, taking place in the full view of the world's population, should have provided undeniable evidence of the truth that God exists, yet it passed and is seen as just another world event; the prophetic evidence diluted into insignificance in the aftermath of World War Two.

Prime Movers

In 1917 Britain was engaged in a terrible war, the *war to end all wars*, the First World War. Unbelievable carnage was taking place daily, and Britain had a huge problem. They were fast running out of explosive material and were in very real danger of losing the war. But God had made a provision that would not only remove the short term explosive problem, but would also start a process that would eventually see the return of the Jews to their homeland, as he had promised years before.

A Jewish scientist by the name of Chaim Weizman, working on new explosives, had discovered the devastating explosive material, TNT, which he offered to the British. This eventually worked into God's plan for Israel.

This timely discovery enabled the allies to *win* the war, but when asked about a reward, Chaim did not ask for wealth or any other personal gain. His request was for nothing other than the provision of a homeland for his people, the Jews. Out of this came the Balfour Declaration on November 2nd 1917, stating primarily that, *her Majesties government will use the best endeavors to facilitate the achievement of this object.*

(statement made in a letter to Arthur Balfour from Lord Rothchild, now in the British museum)

In that same year, the British took over Jerusalem, thus bringing to an end four hundred years of Moorish rule in Palestine. The British commander, General Allenby, out of respect for the king he believed would one day come into the city (Jesus), walked bareheaded into Jerusalem initiating thirty years of British mandate over that much disputed territory.

Theodore Hertzl was also a Jew, who, though trained as a lawyer. took up employment as a news reporter. In Paris he covered the infamous Dreyfuss case. This innocent Jewish, French Army captain was found guilty of treason on the false evidence of anti-sematic fellow officers. But it was that which was taking place outside the courtroom that most affected Hertzl. The crowds were chanting "Death to the Jews!" It was the plural content that shocked him most; for one Jew's alleged crime against the state, all Jews now deserved death. The fragility of his people's acceptance among other nations became vividly clear to him.

So, in 1897 he called together the first Zionist Conference, only to find that, to his amazement, the well-heeled Jews among them gave great opposition to the movement. They felt very safe and secure and well accepted in their chosen societies. Nevertheless, he pressed on with his vision, disappointed but undeterred. History has since revealed the sad deception those European Jews were under, as Hitler's manic drive to exterminate the whole culture became apparent.

It is interesting to note here that Hitler's dream of a Jew-free world was turned on its head as his horrendous activities became another factor in their return to their homeland, and subsequent increase in their population.

Eleazar Ben Yehuda (born Eleazar Pearlman) devoted his life from 1880 until his death in 1922 to the development and modernising of the Hebrew language. He too encountered opposition and scoffing from many of his fellow Jews; reminding me of Noah building his ark miles from any standing water, and in an age when no rain had yet fallen on the Earth. Questions like, *what is the use of an ancient language when everyone speaks the tongue of their adopted land,* would taunt him along with others like, *do you think it will ever be used since we shall never be going back to the land of our fathers?* Yet despite suffering from tuberculosis, he continued with his task, creating a modern version of the old Hebrew, in the belief that his undaunted labours would one day be appreciated. Indeed they have.

It is no coincidence that at a specific time in world history, different individuals in separate locations, together with a particular set of circumstances had become part of a giant historical jigsaw puzzle God was welding this together to bring about the fulfillment of prophesies made thousands of years previously.

The timely invention of Dr Weizman, his selfless request, the passion of Theodore Hertzl for Zion and a return to Israel, Ben Yehuda's unswerving vision for the revival of the Jewish language, World War One, the holocaust of World War Two, the end of Moorish rule in Jerusalem, together with Britain's inept handling of its thirty-year mandate, have all contributed in their own way to that United Nations resolution of 29th of November 1947, for the establishment of the Jewish state. And that is not the end of the story, rather the beginning of an end.

In relation to the Jew's return to their land, and continuing the theme of prophesy fulfilled; we saw earlier that when they were scattered, they were two separated even warring peoples, a northern and a southern kingdom. In a symbolic form the Lord shows Ezekiel that when He brings about their return to the land of their fathers, they will be one people. Ezekiel was told to take two sticks and write on one, *belonging to Judah and the Israelites associated with him*, and on the other, *Ephraim's stick belonging to all the house of Israel associated with him*. God then tells him *to join them together so that they become one stick in your hand*, now let the words written by Ezekiel speak for themselves, remembering that they were penned 2,600 years ago.

Hold before their eyes the sticks you have written on, and say to them this is what the sovereign Lord says: I will take the Israelites out of the nations where they have gone, I will gather them from all around, and bring them back into their own land, I will make them one nation in the mountains of Israel. There will be one King (leader, prime minister) over all of them and they will never again be two nations or divided into two kingdoms. And is it not exactly as it in Israel today? You can read that narrative in Ezekiel 37:16:22. The king referred to is actually, king Jesus.

Another prophesy on the subject of the Jews return to their own land is found in Isaiah, again written some 2,600 years ago. In Isaiah 66:8 the prophet writes this, *who has heard of such a thing? Can a country be born in a Day?"_ "Yet no sooner is Zion in labor than she gives birth to her children.*

That day was May 14th 1948, when the United Nations made the decla--ration of the State of Israel.

The very next day this newly formed nation was attacked by surrounding armies; Egypt, Jordan, Iraq, Syria, and Lebanon. Much planning had gone into this attack long before the nation status of Israel was declared; the only reason possible on the part of the aggressors being to annihilate them before they could get established. Israel was unprepared and ill-equipped to fight against such overwhelming odds; barely three years had passed since many of them had been released from the horrors of the Nazi concentration camps of Europe, and most of them were living in an environment to which they were unaccustomed. The Israelis possessed very little military equipment and in no way did they want this confrontation. The United Nations, (would you believe it) looked the other way; they did nothing whatsoever to intervene in this offence against moral and international justice. It may seem something of an enigma that, having instigated and enabled the return of the Jews to their ancient homeland, God should immediately have them surrounded by openly hostile peoples, but He has a purpose in this.

That war is called Israel's War of Independence. Nearer the truth is that it was their war for survival. The war lasted until March 10th 1949, when finally, Britain petitioned the United Nations to end it because (would you believe) that ill-equipped army were overcoming all the odd's stacked against them and without question, were winning the war.

This unlikely victory, and without intervention a victory it would have been, was a sign to all Earth's people, particularly those who desired the destruction of Israel, that God who had made them a nation would never allow their annihilation. The Israelites are now in their land to stay, no matter what form of aggression is directed at them or no matter how near to extinction they may seem. The most powerful nations on earth may conspire against them, but they will survive. If it has not already been noticed by the unwanted battles they have already had to fight, God's protection over them will be increasingly obvious as we move deeper into this century.

Why do I write this with such confidence? Let me share one more Scripture that tells of God's enduring love for His people. You will find it in Ezekiel 37: 25-28, *They will live in the land I gave my servant Jacob the land where your fathers lived, they and their children and their children's* children will live there forever. *I will make a covenant of peace with them; it will be an everlasting covenant. I will establish them and increase their numbers, and I will put my sanctuary among them forever. My dwelling place will be with them; I will be their God and they will be my people. then the nations will know that I the Lord make Israel holy, when my sanctuary is with them forever.*

I know of only one interpretation of *forever*, and that being so, no way can they be annihilated along the way. And to confirm my own statement of confidence, not one word of that which God has said He will do, has ever failed.

We have seen that the Jewish people were indeed scattered around the whole earth, and gathered back into their own land, all as foretold long before; end of story, job done. Sorry no, just the end of an episode. To really understand the whole council of God, it is needful to realise that the nation of Israel is central to His plans, which involve every individual that has ever lived.

Jesus was sitting one day on the Mount of Olives with his disciples, when they asked him a question. "What shall be the sign of your coming, and of the end of the age?" The answer He gave them is recorded in Mathew 24 and again in Mark 13. In both accounts Jesus refers to a fig tree; symbolic of the nation of Israel.

In Mathew 24:32-33 we read, *now learn this lesson from the fig-tree: as soon as its twigs get tender, and its leaves come out, you know that summer is near. even so, when you see all these things, you know that it is near, right at at the door.*

Here Jesus in His inimitable way employs a parable to convey a profound truth: what He is actually saying is this. Take notice of Israel, apparently cast off by God. The structures of its religious and national institutions are dissipated and scattered to the four corners of the Earth; then watch her re-established as a tender branch back in her old land, putting forth her leaves. If I may use the analogy of photo synthesising and growing stronger as a nation, we should recognise that a time of change is at hand, and almost upon us.

The return of Israel to their land is a significant sign to the people of the Earth that God is moving into a new era, both with Israel and the whole Earth. Many who know their God, feel and sense this, both in their spirit and in the direction of current world events.

CHAPTER FIVE
I Am Written in the Scrolls

There is an expansive reservoir of prophesy relating to the life, ministry, death and resurrection of Jesus Christ, so let us dip into it and further establish the authenticity of the prophesy spoken by God.

The opening words of John's gospel tell us so much about Jesus Christ. *In the beginning was the word, and the word was with God and the word was God, the same was in the beginning with God, by him were all things made and without him was nothing made that was made ... vs 14, the word became flesh and made his dwelling among us.*

These verses clearly tell us that He was the very word of God made flesh. For such an astounding visitation as the word of God living among us here on Earth, you would expect many prophesies to be written, foretelling of His coming; and there are.

He came for a specific purpose that will reveal itself as you read on, this is hinted at in Psalm 40, written some 1,000 years before His birth. *Sacrifice and offering you did not desire; but my ears you pierced, burnt offering and sin offering you did not require. Then said, here I am, I have come - it is written about me in the scrolls.* And indeed, it is.

The first prophesy I want to open up was given to Daniel around 600BC and is recorded in the book of his name, long before Jesus' death on the cross and the final translations of the original Jewish writings. It is often called the prophesy of the seventy weeks; you will find it in Daniel 9:24-

26. It is quite amazing in that with some simple arithmetic, the time of the crucifixion can be calculated. it is necessary that the whole Scripture is quoted in order to follow the reasoning.

Seventy sevens are decreed for your people and your holy city, to finish transgression, and to put an end to sin, to atone for wickedness, to bring in everlasting righteousness, and to seal up vision and prophesy and to anoint the most holy.

Know and understand this: from the issuing of the decree to restore and rebuild Jerusalem until the anointed one, the ruler comes, there will be seven 'sevens'. and sixty-two 'sevens' it will be rebuilt with streets and a trench, but in times of trouble. And after sixty-two 'sevens', the anointed one will be cut off, and will have nothing. the people of the ruler who will come will destroy the city and the sanctuary..

At the time of this prophesy, many of the Jews were in captivity in Babylon, and the restoring and rebuilding here spoken of, relates to a portion of them who were allowed to return to Jerusalem to carry out rebuilding work. The *seventy sevens* here are actually a Jewish measurement called *heptads* and is seventy weeks of years. So, what is being said is, that in seventy weeks of years or four hundred and ninety years, God is going to complete His work on Earth and bring in His everlasting Kingdom. Yes, 2,500 years have passed and it has not happened yet, that is very true, there is also one week not accounted for but we shall look at that later, but now for the calculation giving the date of Jesus' crucifixion.

We are told that from the issuing of the decree, for the Jews to return to Jerusalem to start rebuilding, until the anointed one, Jesus, there would be, seven weeks (49 years) and 62 weeks (434 years), a total of 483 years, Encyclopedia Britannica says the decree to restore and rebuild

Jerusalem was given in 445BC, and the work was completed forty-nine years later; and according to this prophesy the anointed one would be cut off sixty two *heptads* or weeks of years or 434 years after the building work Is completed.

So, we have 49 years to rebuild Jerusalem plus 434 years taking us up to AD38, However, using the Jewish calendar of a 360-day year, we subtract the relevant number of days, and arrive at AD32 as the forecast year of Jesus crucifixion. Sir Robert Anderson, an ex-Scotland Yard police chief has worked out the days as 483 multiplied by 360 days (173,880), and established the date of April 6th AD32 as being the date the *holy one was cut off*.

You may be concerned about the missing week of years in verse 27, which completes the seventy sevens of verse 24, and the total of 490 years. There is in fact, a very large gap between the completion of the 483 years and the start of the final seven.

For the last 2000 years we have been living in what the Church calls the Day of Grace, or the Age of the Church. Previous to the death and resurrection of Jesus, God worked through His people, the Jews. We are now in the age of the New Covenant or Testament when anyone on the planet can approach God through Jesus.

The Jews are now back in their land, which has alerted many Christians to an awareness that God is activating His final plans for the earth. At the end of the age, whenever God decides that to be, He will again work through the Jews, and the missing seven years will begin. Many of the events of those final seven years are written into the book of Revelation, frightening to a great extent in content, and completely indecipherable in terms of time and sequence, though laced with glorious visions of the New Heaven and Earth, and of reconciliation. However, it adds nothing to my proposition that God is, to look into these future promises as there is scant evidence in unfulfilled prophesy.

This prophesy was written into the holy scrolls of the Jews. The whole population would have been familiar with the book of Daniel; to insert this section of the book surreptitiously into every holy document would have been impossible. Jesus did not arrive on Earth unannounced in some mysterious way. Numerous prophesies foretold His coming, written into scrolls known well by the religious leaders of the day, yet during His thirty three years on Earth, including three years of intensive public ministry, they failed to recognise Him for who He was.

In 702BC the prophet Micah foretold that a ruler whose *goings-forth have always been,* would come out of Bethlehem (Micah 5:2), we are all no doubt familiar with the Christmas story, when Herod with cruel intent, gathered all his scribes and priests and asked them where the expected Christ will be born? And they told him Bethlehem, they knew their Scriptures.

Why is there such a problem in accepting these things to be true?

This one event was written 700 years before, known by all the people as the expected birthplace of the Messiah, and impossible to post date. Around 742BC, the prophet Isaiah wrote, *the Lord himself will give you a sign, the virgin will be with child and will give birth to a son, and will call his name Immanuel.* (Isaiah 7:14)

There are incidents in Scripture where we see God enabling old or barren women to have a child, although miraculous, they are not a sign. But for a young woman who had never known a man to bare a child, that is a sign not only for the Jews of the time, but for all that care to consider it.

It is interesting to note that Mary, the young woman in question, had a cousin who was also pregnant, but in her old age,. This, too, had been foretold by Isaiah. *The voice of him that cry's in the wilderness, prepare the way of the Lord, make straight in the desert a highway for our God* (Isaiah 40:3 KJV) Mary's cousin, Elizabeth's, son was John the Baptist, who as the gospels tell us he did just that, he preached in the desert about getting right with God. (see Matthew 3:1)

The whole unity of the Scriptures never ceases to thrill me. I once heard an excited believer of another faith state on television that, "the Bible is a hotchpotch of ideas cobbled together." Nothing could be further from the truth . There is a solid core of inseparable continuity running through its entire volume, binding thousands of years of history together, even down to the genealogies of the Jewish peoples, way back to Adam.

Having dipped briefly into prophesies of the time, place and manner of Jesus' coming, let us have a look now at some of those statements concerning his life and death. Around 520BC, the prophet, Zechariah, wrote these words, *rejoice greatly O daughter of Zion; shout daughter of Jerusalem; see your King comes to you, righteous and having salvation; gentle and riding on a donkey, on a colt the foal of a donkey.* (Zechariah 9:9)

Zechariah was predicting the occasion we now refer to as Palm Sunday, when Jesus rode into Jerusalem in exactly that manner. Some may say coincidence, or that Jesus did that to comply with the Scriptures, that certainly can be argued, but set among so many other foretold instances, all taking place within a few days of each other, those arguments grow increasingly weaker. (Luke 19:19-30)

The price received by Judas for betraying Jesus, thirty pieces of silver, was also foretold by Zechariah. (11:12-13) He also told that those same coins would be used to buy the Potter's field, where, according to Acts 1:18-20, Judas died a terrible death. The field was renamed, The Field of Blood. 1000 years before Christ, King David wrote Psalm 22:14-18 - a psalm that portrays so graphically the agonising death of someone nailed to a cross, also including other specific things that took place at Jesus' crucifixion.

I am poured out like water, all my bones are out of joint, my heart has turned to wax it has melted within me, my strength is dried up like a potsherd, and my tongue sticks to the roof of my mouth, you lay me in the dust of death, dogs have surrounded me, evil men have encircled me, they have pierced my hands and my feet, I can count all my bones, people stare and gloat over me, they divide my garments among them and cast lots for my clothing.

Written, as I said, 1,000 years before Christ, long before the completed cannon of the Jewish scriptures in 246BC, and impossible to have been *slipped* unnoticed into the original scrolls at a later date. There is no record anywhere of anyone surviving crucifixion, and only someone that experienced firsthand that awful death, could have given so experiential an account.

David, the writer, did not suffer crucifixion, and I propose that there is only one that could, and He lives to describe the horrors of it; He lives outside of time where past, present and future are one, and He, by His spirit, gave David that insight. A potty proposition? Let us not lose sight of the fact that we are dealing with the supernatural. .What do you make of the last few words of our previous Scripture, *they divide my garments among them and cast lots for my clothing?*

In Mark 15-24 we read in his first-hand account, *and they crucified Jesus dividing up his clothes, they cast lots to see what each would get.* The

Roman soldiers doing this would have had no knowledge of the Jewish scriptures, but were simply doing what they always did to profit from the executions. The reason why they had to cast lots for his main garment was that it was woven in one piece and would have been destroyed had they divided it.

There was a modicum of compassion shown to Roman crucifixion victims. In Psalm 69:20-21, also written around 1000 years before Christ, we read more of how Jesus felt. *Scorn has broken my heart; and left me helpless; I looked for sympathy, but there was none; for comforters but I found none. they put gall in my food and gave me vinegar for my thirst.* This was also offered to Jesus to ease the pain but He refused.

In 712BC, the prophet Isaiah wrote an incredibly poignant account of the suffering of Jesus. Isaiah 53 contains references to His death, His silence before His accusers, the reason He had to die, and much more.

With all of these Scriptural readings, I do not want to lose sight of the reason for these Scriptures, which is to place before you irrefutable evidence that God is, and as He has provided so great a reservoir of prophesy fulfilled, it is from there that I draw my reasoning.

Back to Isaiah 53. As we look into it, keep in mind that it was not written after the event, but 712 years before it. *He is despised and rejected of men; a man of sorrows and familiar with suffering. Like one from whom men hide their faces, he was despised, and we esteemed him not, surely, he took up our infirmities and carried our sorrows, yet we considered him stricken by God, smitten by him and afflicted but he was pierced for our transgressions, he was crushed for our iniquities: the punishment that brought us peace was upon him; and by his wounds we are healed.*

Verse 7 foretells of how Jesus amazed his inquisitors in that He offered no words that could have averted the obvious fate that awaited Him, this is recorded in Mark 15:4-5

Verse 8 speaks of Jesus' demise. *He was cut off out of the land of the living.* His death by crucifixion is well documented in all four gospels

Verse 9 tells us He *made His grave with the wicked, and with the rich in His death.* Mathew 27:57-60 tells us that a rich man, Joseph of Arimathea, gave his own grave in which to lay the body of Jesus.

Verse 12 tells of His companions in death, *He was numbered with the transgressors.* Jesus was hung on a cross with two thieves, one either side, and both Mathew 27:38 and Luke 23:33 verify this.

It is extremely doubtful that Isaiah, or for that matter any of the prophets, had a full understanding of the things God had caused them to write. Even the disciples were for most of Jesus' ministry, very unclear about the ultimate purpose of His visitation here on Earth. Many Scriptures speak of it, but the Isaiah 53 tells it clearly, in fact the whole of that chapter, apart from the incidental prophesies we have just looked into, is dedicated to the theme of the Messiah and His death.

I include two verses that embrace this theme, with the recommendation that you read the entire chapter for yourself.

But he was pierced for our transgressions, he was crushed for our iniquities: the punishment that brought us peace was upon him; and with his wounds we are healed. we all like sheep, have gone astray; each one of us has turned to his own way; and the Lord has laid on him the iniquity of us all. (Isaiah 53:5-6)

When talking of the revelation of foretold events, the promise of our reconciliation to God through the death of His son, Jesus, as written throughout the Bible, is second to none, and it has been fulfilled.

There is one further prophesy I want to share concerning the crucifixion of Jesus because it totally eradicates the notion that He survived the ordeal.

We are told in John 19:34 that a soldier thrust his spear into Jesus' side after he had broken the legs of the other two men crucified either side of Him. This common practise was to hasten their death; robbed of the ability to use their legs in order to push to breath, they would quickly suffocate. But the soldier in question found that Jesus was already dead of His own volition. He had *given up the ghost*, but to make certain, the Roman soldier thrust his spear into the side of Jesus at the point he knew would guarantee death. This refutes the notion that Jesus survived His ordeal on the cross. It has to be more than coincidence that written hundreds of years before the events had taken place, not one event has failed to be totally accurately predicted. The organisation involved in attempting to post date any Old Testament Scriptures is unthinkable, especially immediately after Jesus' resurrection.

The ruling religious establishment of the time was very hostile to (in their opinion) the preposterous claims of the followers of Jesus that He had risen from the dead. The consideration that His followers could have written these prophesies into the ancient scrolls, is too ridiculous to even consider.

Immediately after Jesus' death and resurrection, the ruling religious authorities set out to eradicate any possibility of the propagation of His teachings. His followers, now called Christians, were under constant surveillance and fear for their lives and liberty. A situation that increased considerably during the early centuries of Christianity, and is still very prevalent in many countries today.

Stephen was the first to die; stoned to death. Saul of Tarsus who became Paul the apostle after his Damascus road experience, minded the jackets of those who threw the stones, Peter and John were thrown into prison, Andrew was crucified on a Saint Andrew cross, Peter was crucified upside down in Rome, James was beheaded by Herod, Bartholomew is believed to have been flogged to death in Armenia, and tradition has it that James the younger was crucified in Egypt.

Paul, who had been complicit in the death of Stephen, was imprisoned many times, and five times received thirty lashes from the Jews, and was beaten with rods on three occasions, and is believed to have been executed by Nero, the Roman emperor.

Countless faceless followers of Jesus suffered similar fates at the hands of the Jewish religious leaders of Israel or Rome in those early years. Many were dipped in tar and burned to illuminate Nero's rose gardens, or died fighting gladiators for public entertainment.

With your life in the hands of those who hate the doctrine you represent; would you be ready to perpetuate that which you knew to be a lie? They were prepared to die because they knew it to be the truth.

CHAPTER SIX
Not a Species

What is it that sets mankind apart from all other living things on the planet? The Bible makes it very clear every time God created a living entity, He said, *let there be...*, and it was. He also said of it that it was to be, *according to its kind*. The first was to show the power of His spoken word: some instances of which we have looked at in prophesy, the second saying, *according to its kind* was to ensure His creations perpetuated in the form in which He had designed it.

We are all no doubt familiar with the DNA coding present in every living thing, in which its whole structure, in fact every detail of its being, is written. Everything created is in the form that fits in precisely with the delicate eco system God had established on Earth, and except where man has tried, no natural blending of species will ever take place.

But, the creation of man was on a very different scale. First was the Godhead's decision: Genesis 1:26, *let us make man in our image, in our likeness and let them rule over...all created things.*

In verse 27 we are then told that God created us in His own image, and that He created us male and female. With man, there it was no single sentence, *let there be.* I do not want to quote all the relevant verses, but God gave to us specific instructions. First off, He blessed us and told us to be fruitful and multiply and replenish the Earth. Then He gave us dominion over every other thing that moved on the face of the Earth and He gave us every herb and fruit for our food. (Genesis 9:3-4) It was not until sometime after the flood that we became carnivorous.

At this point you may be thinking, it is all very well you quoting these Scriptures, but where does the ascent of man fit into all this? The truth is it does not. This is an issue I have to address, so let us start by considering the ape-to-man transition of evolutionary theory.

An investigation reported in the journal, Nature, volume 405, pp983-925 published on June 22, 2002, confirms we shared 98.4% of our DNA with an ape. This seemed to prove the authenticity of our ape ancestry, however, the investigation was incomplete and now the figure is placed at 94%, which again seem to uphold the evolutionist claims. So, let us look into it.

Most of us are familiar with the double helix form of DNA, the simple illustration is of an elongated twisted ladder, where the rungs consist of sugar phosphates. These half rungs are called nucleotides, they are *adenine*, thymine, guanine and cytosine. Adenine can only combine with thymine and guanine only with cytosine as they come together to form full *rungs* forming the full ladder arrangement. These half rungs or nucleotides of which there around 3.2 billion in the human genome, by their exact pairing, dictate the entire complexity of each individual's construction.

We it seems, share 94% of our DNA with an ape, that is a 6% difference. Therefore, as there are 3.5 billion nucleotides in our genome and each pairing has a bearing on our sharing, we have 192 million that we do not share, which equates to a considerable number of potential differences?

It seems that we have evolved over many millions of years, having had a series of ape-like ancestors along the way, ignoring our earlier forefathers, amoeba.

Most people are unaware that nowhere on Earth has there ever been found bona fide remains of a creature transitory twixt ape and man. For 150 years now the search has continued on many sites in many countries, and all have eventually been identified as either fully man or fully ape. Evolutionists are really desperate; they need evidence to bolster their threadbare theory.

Even the planets are scrutinised for some modicum of evidence of life in whatever form it might exist, or has existed. Even if it wallows in sulphuric acid, it is able to prove that living organisms can evolve without the hand of God. Without such evidence, their theory remains just that, and one has to admire a faith that dogmatically holds fast to the unproveable. As if to add to their frustrations, it is not only man's evolution that is unproven, but that of every other living thing on the planet. All have shown to have been fully developed as we encounter them today throughout the fossil strata, and despite many educated attempts to show otherwise, all remain in the form in which they were created.

From your school days you may remember the famous line-up of ape to man, from a stooping baboon-like creature to modern man walking off the end of the page. Over the years their authenticity has been burst like soap bubbles; the whole concept is degrading to man and offensive to God. This idea of ape becoming man, first envisaged by Charles Darwin, was given the name pithecanthropus before it had been found. This term was made up out of two Greek words, *Pithekos* meaning ape and *Anthropos* meaning man, and having imagined him, they set out to find him.

Among the early finds was the infamous Piltdown Man, found near Lewis in East Sussex, UK in 1912. This alledged 500 000-year-old fossil was expertly put together from an ape jaw bone, a tooth and other bits and pieces, and handed over to qualified paleontologists as a genuine find, part man, part ape.

When viewed as a student-type prank, it can be laughed at as a harmless joke, but this was not the case. This fraud was inspected by many qualified to do so, and was declared to be genuine. With teeth filed to deceive, an ape's tooth and an ape jaw it should not have been too difficult for experts to spot a fraud, yet it was not until 1953, forty years later, that it was publicly recognised for what it was; the British Museum being involved throughout.

This fraudulent object was actively used to further the erroneous notion of man's decent from ape during forty critical years of deceitful propagation. If it was innocent, why did the perpetrators not admit it?

Hesperopithecus, more simply known as Nebraska Man, consisted of one single tooth, from which the London Illustrated News on 24th of June 1922, published a full-page picture of a naked, very primitive ape-man and woman.

Meanwhile in America, in 1925, a senator, William Bryan, was campaigning against children being taught that they were descendent from apes. In court this enhanced single tooth was the *star witness* against his motion, and yes, the atheists won the case. However, in 1927, the single tooth was found to be that of an extinct pig. Was there a re-trial? No way. Incidentally, at that time Piltdown Man was still twenty six years away from exposure and still contributing to the ape-to-man deceit.

Eugene Dubois was an ambitious young Dutch surgeon, the finder of Java Man, or *pithecanthropus erectus*, and a lecturer in anatomy at Amsterdam University. He wanted to get to the far East to follow his passion to find evidence of early man, so he enlisted in the Dutch East Indian Army and was posted to Java, where near the village of Wadjak, he found skulls that were found to be human. He hid these for thirty years. Then in central Java in 1892, in the bank of the river Solo, his expedition found two teeth and part of a skull cap. In 1893, 15 meters from where the skull was found, an upper thigh bone was discovered: so was born Java Man. 300 000 years old, said the strata in which they were found, however, that is another story.

Eugene's finds were much disputed. He intimated four years before he died that he considered them to be the remains of a giant gibbon. So far, no *link* bones only *wish* bones.

I just love Neanderthal man, I find him so interesting, I love the story of how he got his name. Near Dusseldorf in Germany there is a beautiful valley and often this young Christian man would walk there and commune with God. He would compose hymns and sing them out loud. He died at an early age, just thirty years old. He lived from 1650 until 1680 and his love for the valley caused the locals to name it after him, his name is Joachim Neander, so it became the Neander valley. Many years later when excavation work was being carried out in that valley, and they unearthed a skeleton, considering it to be a new find in man's transitory story, it was given the name of the place in which it was found: so Neanderthal man was born.

I know it adds nothing, but I find it pleasing in a quirky sort of way that the first verse of Neander's most well-known hymn begins with the words: *Praise to the Lord the almighty (the king of creation)*. Many more Neanderthals have been found since that first one in Germany.

Unfortunately, in order to give him a more transitory appearance, he was at first depicted as a stooped hairy large primitive sub human, however, that one, and some others were subsequently found to be old and suffering from arthritis and rickets. True he has large bones and was heavily muscular, but you will find at least one of a similar structure in the front row of any top class rugby team.

It is seldom mentioned that Neanderthal man had a larger brain than the rest of us. Does that mean we are less advanced? Throughout the world we see different sizes and colours of humanity; some groups smaller, others taller, and so it is with Neanderthal. Dress him in today's clothes and he would not stand out as any different in a crowd.

Cro-Magnon man is another find that has no reason to be called pre-historic, found in Les Eyzies in France; these families were cave dwellers who brightened up their dwellings by painting colourful pictures of animals on the walls. They possessed no transitory features, indeed they were truly human. It would seem the only reason they were considered non-human is that they lived in caves.

Not eight miles from where I live, people were living in caves into the 20th century. That does not make them cavemen in the evolutionary sense, nor does it these people. *Ramapithecus* was drawn as a full-size figure with long arms, standing in a semi stooped position covered in hair having an ape like face. The whole imaginary figure conceived from thirty pieces of jaw and teeth.

The skull of *Zinjanthropus boisei* better known as *Australopithecus boisei* was made up from 100 small pieces found in 1959, and subsequently drawn with several totally different faces. One for the Sunday Times, April 5th 1964, one for the Illustrated London News, 9th January 1960, one drawn for *origins* by Richard Leaky and R Lewin in 1977, and one for the British Museum: each is so distinctly different that no mutual feature can be found.

Pekin man consists of broken pieces of ape's skull and jaws, from which using a great deal of plaster four skulls were constructed, then using a jaw found 80 feet higher in the excavation they constructed another of a woman's skull and they called it, *Nellie*.

Homo Habilis was found in Africa by Richard Leaky, and estimated to be 2.8 million years old, but there is a problem there. Though it is more human in appearance, it pre dated its ape-like members by 2.5 million years, and despite the finder's own recognition that it is human-like, artists still drew it looking distinctly ape-like. So it remains contentious, in that he was found in the wrong strata, according to the geological column.

This column, with which all are no doubt familiar, shows the Earth's strata together with the age associated with each together with another chart showing the life forms you would find in each stratum. However, there is no known reliable dating of each individual stratum, nor indeed the strict evidence of life-forms in that order found in it. It is a concept born out of the notion that all things are as they always were, and that is not so.

Much evidence shows that our Earth has had many geological manipulating catastrophes. This geological column gives rise to the system known as circular reasoning. This is how it works. The fossil you found is dated by the strata in which it was found, and the rock by the fossil found in it. Unfortunately, things turn up that put a spanner in the works. For instance, human remains that turn up in coal seams supposedly millions of years old, or rocks of a much younger age than the coal seam. Such remains are usually treated as a hoax or simply ignored. But this is stuff that fits perfectly into the catastrophic worldwide flood of Noah, where all in the path of those huge waves and tsunamis would be swept along in it and deposited in totally haphazard heaps, to be covered by every subsequent wave. There are numerous such finds hidden away as they are thorns in the side of evolution.

The whole theory of evolution depends absolutely on vast periods of time, and indeed, as we look at the world around us, great mountain ranges spectacular rock formations and deep gorges through which racing rivers run, our obvious reaction is to consider that countless ages alone could have formed them. I want to place before you some thoughts on that a little later.

At one time people marveled at the wonderful works of God, until this new religion with its scientific (?) answer to all things provided a seemingly more satisfactory understanding. The reason for the question mark by scientific, is that as you may have already gleaned from some of the above illustrations, some scientists deviate from the true course of their profession in order to preserve the philosophy or to obtain a name. Question the great age concept and the whole thing falls apart, how are these figures arrived at?

Radio metric dating methods utilise the known decay times of various unstable elements, uranium lead, potassium argon and carbon 14. The first two are used to ascertain the greater periods of time, carbon 14 has a half life of 5730 years. Throughout our lifetimes every living thing, including ourselves, absorbs this element. When we die, our intake ceases, and the decay period can be calculated.

Carbon14 is formed by interaction with other particles within the atmosphere, such as neutrons and nitrogen, however, the calculations are dependent upon a constant condition, and many things could contribute to an incorrect count. If we recognise the pre-flood situation, where the world was shrouded by the water canopy, every fossil found would give a very misleading calculation of the age of the subject under investigation, that would lead to an apparent far greater age for all pre-flood finds.

The same applies to both uranium lead and potassium argon. We may know their half-lives, but if all things have not been constant from the time the investigated rock was laid down, you are working on an assumed presumption. Several conditions can contribute to error, heat is one, a leaching out of the element is another, except you know the complete story of an investigated rock, a history of many alleged millions of years, your assumption is that all things have been constant since its layering.

Dinosaurs, now they are a mystery, earth pre-flood would have been their dream environment, predominantly vegetarian, in an ideal temperature, low level solar particles, high level oxygen, perfect for long life and large growth. The mystery is in their demise, why not the flood that eliminated all other life? Followed by a changed atmosphere that would no longer be able to sustain them.

Though laughed at by so many, the flood of Noah fits Earth's investigations like a glove. Wherever or whenever items are found, of any strata or species, no problem. After that worldwide catastrophe, we would expect to find, animals and humans in a disorganised and random burial situation; exactly what we do find, as the tumultuous waters destroyed forests, re-shaped Earths geology, and swept all before them. We have all been fed the idea that the flood was only localised, and our concept is of a continual steady rainfall, when it was the most disastrous ever recorded in Earth's history.

I have heard many TV commentators talking of Noah's flood in dismissive terms, citing the many folklore stories referring to local floods. Hence the worldwide myth of a worldwide flood. Have they not considered the reason so many such stories abound within so many diverse peoples? It is because these stories have been handed down from generation to generation, starting with Shem, Ham and Japheth, the sons of Noah, from whom everyone on Earth has descended. Therefore, why should it not be true? The answer is written within the true geographic chart; Earth itself.

With an acceptance of a flood-geology, there is no deceit necessary when a fossil does not fit into the age of a strata in which it was found. No problem emerges when a human skull turns up in an allegedly fifty million year old coal seam. Those individuals would have been caught up in the torrent, carrying in it debris including masses of trees ripped out by the roots, until finally depositing its load where the miners found it, covered by subsequent deposits of rock etc. The vegetation then turns to coal leaving not only the skull but other flora and fauna buried within it. Incidentally, this creates just the conditions required for coal to form: heat and pressure.

The Flood is not as *nutty Noah and Nelly* as many are led to believe. One great hurdle stands in the way of an honest investigation into the authenticity of this biblical account; the realisation that God is. Earlier on, when looking into the methods of dating strata, I mentioned that I had some thoughts to share on the whole subject of creation and this seems a good place to do it.

When considering questions involving time, such as the age of the Earth or the ages of planets and such, it is important for us to recognise that our earth-bound, finite minds consider all these questions in terms of time. It is impossible for us not to do so, we are locked in time. Almighty

God is spirit, He is eternal, He inhabits a timeless dimension, and when He, from outside time, created the heavens and the Earth, He created time itself.

Therefore, that which God envisaged and spoke into being would be in the form and condition in which He conceived it. He could have created it in a form that required an ageing process, or He could have created it in the condition in which we find it today. According to His own account in Genesis, God carried out an instant, six-day creation, and all things were formed as we recognise them now. As Almighty God, it is His prerogative to create however He chooses, and if our time-tethered minds are unable to assimilate this, that is our problem. In recognising those things; a six-day creation by an Almighty God, from His timeless eternity, should hold no problems for those that believe that He is.

Once I understood this, my years of battling with the authenticity and reliability of radiometric dating, the geological chart and such receded into insignificance as I relaxed in the knowledge that God does things His way. I want now to share another major prophesy showing that God not only reveals to us the future, but also that they are always 100% accurate.

CHAPTER SEVEN
This King was a Head of Gold

For many, the stories written in the Bible should be pre-fixed, *once upon a time*, because they seem so out of touch with the age in which we live. People's way of life, the apparent disregard for life, that a conquering King could without mercy put out the eyes of the defeated foe, life in so many ways different to ours. However, people were no less human and alive to every emotion we all experience.

In 607BC, Nebuchadnezzar, king of Babylon, modern day Iraq, besieged Jerusalem scattering many Jews out of their land, and carrying away to his own country the young and intelligent to be taught the language and ways of the Chaldeans. These captive were to be made useful to the King in administrative offices with their knowledge and wisdom.

Among them was a young man named Daniel, you find his story in the book of the same name. I paraphrase Daniel 2 below.

Nebuchadnezzar had a dream one night and although he could not remember it, he was greatly troubled by it, so much so that he gathered all his Chaldean wise men and expected them to tell him of it They told him that unless he could tell them the dream, they were unable to give him the interpretation. This made the king extremely angry, so much so that he ordered that they be put to death and their houses reduced to rubble. These were the top men in the country, and Daniel and his friends were included although they were not present at that meeting with the king. Arioch, the kings captain, began rounding up all the wise men in Babylon, and when he came for Daniel and his friends, Daniel asked Arioch to approach the king to grant him an audience. This was duly arranged and Daniel asked Nebuchadnezzar for time to seek his God for an answer to the king's request, this was granted. Daniel and his friends held what we would term as prayer meetings and God answered Daniel in a night vision.

Having received the answer for the king from God, Daniele was granted another audience with him.

He began by telling Nebuchadnezzar that the dream concerned what should be in the latter days.

(My paraphrase Daniel 2:31-16) *What you saw in your dream was a great image of a man, the head was made of gold, the breast and arms were of silver, his belly and his thighs of brass and his legs were of iron, his feet and toes were part iron and part clay, and as you looked at it, a stone that was not cut out by hands struck the image on its feet of iron and clay, and smashed it into many small pieces, and the wind carried them away never to be seen again, then the stone that had struck the image became a great mountain and filled the whole Earth.* (Daniel 2:31-35)

Immediately after telling king Nebuchadnezzar of his dream, Daniel continued to give the interpretation of it.

(My paraphrase Daniel 2:36-44) *You, Nebuchadnezzar are the head of gold, the God of heaven has given you all your power and authority, after you will come another kingdom inferior to you, then another of brass shall rule the Earth, after that shall come a fourth kingdom strong as iron, and just as iron breaks in pieces, so will this kingdom be, this kingdom shall be divided, and just as iron and clay will not mix, neither will these, and as you saw the stone cut out without hands completely destroying the various parts of the image never to be seen again, so God is going to set up a kingdom that shall never be destroyed, it will consume all other kingdoms and it will stand for ever.*

The king was placated and immediately exalted Daniel to high office, though Daniel had made it clear to the king that it was his God that had provided the information and it was not of himself.

This is not just a nice little story but an amazing prophesy as we shall see; history has revealed its accuracy.

Nebuchadnezzar was indeed a powerful King of once mighty Babylon, and indeed, gold was well chosen as symbolic of its reign. It was commonplace in his household, most taken from the peoples he had conquered. History confirms that his kingdom ruled from 605BC until 539BC.

Then followed the Medo Persian empire, two peoples joined as one, as are the two arms joined at the breast. They were noted for their liberal use of silver, and history records their reign from 539BC to 331BC. Then along comes Alexander the Great with his army, they are the thighs of brass, inferior in wealth to the Persians, but militarily more powerful. History records Alexander's untimely death and the dividing of his kingdom between his four generals. This Greek empire lasted from 331BC to 168BC.

The iron rule of Rome took the place of Greece, with their iron swords and iron discipline, dividing eventually into an East and West empire, as depicted by the two legs of the image. This longest lasting of all the kingdoms ruled from 168BC until AD476.

This dream of Nebuchadnezzar does not end with Rome but continues to tell of Kingdoms and events far into the future. Yes, our future and that of our descendants. The kingdoms of the feet of iron mixed with clay and its ten toes, is unidentifiable with any kingdom following on from Rome, just as there is a gap in the prophesy of the seventy weeks we looked at earlier. It seems we have the same situation here, these kingdoms or group of nations, a union of some sort will certainly take its place on the world stage at some point.

There is much speculation on the subject. One predominating line of thought is that the feet of clay and iron is the continuation of the legs of iron: the European Union was formed under the treaty of Rome. Daniel 9:26 speaks of *the people of the ruler that shall come, will destroy the city and the sanctuary* as the Romans did under Titus in AD70. The tenuous bonding of the nations under the EU flag is leading many to consider this alliance to be the subject matter?

Although the *ten toes* pose a challenge, as EU membership already exceeds that number. However, numbers in the Bible have considerable significance. Ten Indicates the full measure of human responsibility, as with the ten commandments and the parable of the ten talents, it may or may not be that those nations formed under the treaty of Rome, are this kingdom. One thing is certain, such a kingdom will reign on Earth in the latter days. The 100% accuracy of all other fulfilled prophesies confirm this, and I would add that many scholars have ended up with egg on their face as a result of incorrect interpretations of Scripture. Complete understanding of God's forecasts can only be seen in their fulfillment.

Among all speculation concerning expected events in these last days, the whole Christian church is united on the last part of that prophesy. Daniel 2:44 states that *in the time of those kings, the God of heaven will set up a Kingdom that will never be destroyed: nor will it be left to another people. It will crush all those kingdoms and bring them to an end, but it will itself endure forever.* The *stone cut out without hands* is Jesus Christ who Himself will break the powers of all these nations and rule as king in God's everlasting kingdom.

If ever there was a period in the history of Earth's governments when the necessity for an intervention by its creator was needed, it is this period in which we are living. You do not need to be a sage or an enlightened philosopher to discern the confusion, international mistrust, financial insecurity, reluctance to carry out planet-saving policies because of greed or personal esteem, moral decline even at governmental levels, millions starving or living in terrible conditions, while their leaders live in luxury, government backed religious intolerance, and so much more.

The whole of the dream's interpretation, forecasts the failure of successive world governments. As mentioned, the *stone not cut out by hands* is the Lord Jesus Christ. He is that which became a mountain that filled the whole Earth, and the government that He will form will be like no other world authority. It will be firmly based on, honesty, truth, righteousness, morality, love, temperance, faith, goodness, joy, peace, and gentleness.

His kingdom here on Earth will last for one thousand years, when there will be a new heaven and a new Earth. Why wait for a thousand years? Believe it or not, even under such a leadership as described above, many will rebel and prefer life as their forefathers knew it, so there will be a final refining in the end when those vestiges of impurity will be dealt with. Only then can the new heaven and the new Earth come into being. It is all written in the book of Revelation.

Moving away from creation, evolution and prophetic infallibility questions, into something quite different, yet coming at the same considerations from an indirect angle: still proving that God is, I want to share with you an experience endured by my wife and myself that has had a profound effect on our lives. It says much about the existence of a spiritual realm, and that all we can see and feel and recognise with our human senses, is not all that there is.

CHAPTER EIGHT
Fifty-two Days

In all of us there is a mental void into which we dump the things that frustrate our logic, a luxury unavailable to those who experience the seemingly unexplainable. To stumble into a world where reality recedes into insignificance, the impossible becomes the norm, and all that you have ever believed or disbelieved, is turned on its head by an invisible force too powerful to resist, was the nightmare Carol and I were surreptitiously drawn into on Christmas day in 1968.

That was the day the seed was planted as prior to then, we had never even heard of the Ouija board game. There were about ten people around the dining room table in the house of a neighbour, the letters of the alphabet arranged in a circle, and some had their index fingers on an upturned wine glass, that moved erratically around the circle to the accompaniment of drink-lubricated laughter, interspersed with debates about who was and who was not, pushing it.

The following day, having eaten an oversize dinner, we decided to have a go at the game, we prepared the table as at the party, adding the words *yes* and *no* opposite each other. Carol's father wanted no part it, but her sister was up for it. Fingers on glass we waited for something to happen, but nothing did, then one of us asked the question, "is anybody there?" A short hesitation then with our fingers on board it moved towards *yes*.

Carol's sister screamed and ran from the room, Cyril laughed, "Don't be daft it's those two they are pushing it"

"Are you pushing it?" I asked Carol

"No", she replied, "are you?"

"No" I replied truthfully.

We managed to persuade Carol's sister to return to the table, the same question was asked, the glass moved and her sister ran again. Wild horses would not have dragged her back.

Carol and I continued to play the game on our own. "Right", said Cyril, "let's see if there really is anybody there." He lit up a Cigarette. "You two face away from me and I want that glass to tell me when I put this cigarette to my mouth." With fingers on the glass we waited for It to move, then suddenly, taking us both by surprise, it dashed over to *yes*.

"You must have been looking", said Cyril. We did the cigarette thing several times; we did not cheat and the glass was right every time. We were now quite convinced that something was there, that is Carol and I were, Carol's sister was still unhappy about it and Cyril was still sceptical. The logical next step was to ask, "Who is there"? The answer stunned us into silence: *Nan Bennet*.

Carol's grandmother had passed away two years before and many of her childhood years had been spent living with her in Summercourt in Cornwall. There had been a loving and caring relationship between them.

After recovering from the shock, we returned to the game and asked her the obvious questions, where are you now and what is it like? The reply via the moving glass was that she was in heaven and all was wonderful. And so, it began, little did we realise at that time, how much we had to learn about the power that moved the glass.

Carol and I were an ordinary couple, with two daughters almost six and three, with problems common to most young parents. I was working a three-shift system at a Wolverhampton factory, and on returning from morning shift the day after our first encounter with the glass, I was met by a very excited Carol, telling me she had been playing the game on her own and Nan Bennet had told her of things way back in her childhood. We became well and truly hooked, every spare moment was spent on the *chat li*ne to Nan Bennet, until one evening, totally unexpectedly, the glass told us, *God is listening*.

Now this was a big setback for me, talking to a deceased grandmother was one thing but this really was something else, I, an evangelical atheist, had been communicating with a dead person for several weeks, and despite my hostile stance that there was no life after death, I had not been fazed by this. Why? Any theories I may have considered were not only dissipated but disintegrated far sooner than I could possibly have imagined. We continued to spend the majority of our spare time talking to Nan Bennet, growing accustomed to the fact that God was listening, and occasionally *she* would say, "God is telling me to ask you a question."

Suddenly one night the glass took on a frightening new personality. "God is here", it announced, moving around the nine letters with such ferocity we could hardly keep our fingers on it. Playtime was now well and truly over. The new voice wasted no time in establishing its dominance over the glass, Carol and myself. *What can you see, Carol?* was spelt out at breakneck speed, it seems that in her mind's eye Carol saw a figure in a long black cloak, and she told Him what she could see.

What am I holding?

"You are holding a large black book with a chain and a bunch of keys hanging from it ...John's name is in this book"

The glass was rapidly spelling something out and though I cannot recall the exact words used, I was told very clearly that my afterlife destination was *Hell*. I would have to pay the consequence for my lifestyle and rejection of Him.

Can you possibly imagine the immediate effect this had on me? The total despair and utter hopelessness? I had been told by God, the ultimate and absolute universal authority, in whom until that moment I had not believed, that my eternity in hell was inescapable.

So began my indescribable nightmare, death, the ultimate way out of unbearable human problems was now the entrance into that which is unthinkable.

Carol was undergoing a completely different experience. She could do no wrong, whilst I was relegated to a finger on the glass, she was enjoying out of body experiences and pleasant conversations with this God. I began to have multi colored nightmares filled with mocking cartoon-like characters, making sleep an undesirable thing. Most nights I spent kneeling by the bed asking God to forgive me and to rub my name out of that book.

About that time, God began to do a new thing with us. Moving the glass, He would ask us, "What am I saying?" We then had to listen to our thoughts and answer from the words most dominant in our minds. If we were correct, the glass would swing to *yes*, if not it would spell out, *No, listen again*, until we got it right. We realised only later that we had two levels of thought, our own mental processes and the *voice* of God, the latter becoming more and more commanding. The structure for confusion and mental instability was being established, but always there was the glass to return to where any confusion could be sorted out.

Then came that incredible night when He said He had something very important to talk to us about, it concerned a task we would have to undertake for Him. He said the time had now come for His son to be born into the world, and that Carol would have this child. I have every sympathy with those people who at this moment are thinking *enough is enough*, sensing they are now entering into some figment of a contorted imagination. No one, least of all someone so easily embarrassed as myself, deliberately sets out to court ridicule. All these situations are told exactly as Carol and I experienced them, nothing added or expanded, quite the opposite, there are details we both intend to keep to ourselves

I was told that I would play no part in this conception and Carol herself would be unaware that it had taken place, though on the night of its alleged occurrence, God's presence was very evident in the room. Carol was told that she would no longer be able to drink alcohol or smoke. Drink was no problem, she did little of that, but smoking was a different matter. For some time Carol had been trying to give it up but could not, until the morning after the visitation, she lit up, took one draw that tasted so disgusting that she threw it away and has never smoked since. If God were to visit you today and tell you He would pick your lottery numbers for you, how would you feel, euphoric? You bet. We were told this child must have the very best up-bringing money and education can buy. We obviously were unable to provide this, so God would make wealth available to us.

There was no national lottery in those days and the only hope most working people had of becoming instantly rich was by winning the football pools. I used to play them regularly until I had the magic eight draws up and could not fit them into the plan, so I gave up on it. "You obtain a pools coupon", said God, "and I will tell you which teams are going to draw on Saturday". God may hate me, and I am certain of going to hell, but boy my lifestyle was about to change.

The pools agent at the factory was *The Weasel*, whose appearance accounted for his nickname. He spent most of his time drinking at a pub called The Eagle, and whenever I saw him, the words of a song always came into my mind,

Up and down the city road,
in and out of The Eagle,
that's the way the money goes,
pop goes the weasel.

So I contacted The Weasel and arranged for a copy to be dropped off for me. Strangely the promise of wealth did little to ease the growing frustrations, and my dreams were no less frightening, sometimes previewing situations occurring days later. One night I was told by the other voice that my soul was so filthy that it would have to be removed to be cleaned. Unbelievable, *yes*; what kind of an idiot was I to go along with all of this stuff? But the reality is that my self-confidence and logical reasoning had been eroded by this dominating God personality. I was putty in its grip. Immediately I found I could no longer laugh or cry. I had become void of emotion, and that condition was on-going.

Another perplexing factor had now entered into what remained of my ability for sensible thought, adding further turmoil to my increasingly weary brain cells, and it was this: though I had no time for religion, I had in common with most a basic knowledge of the Christmas story. How Mary had a child not conceived through Joseph to whom she was engaged, that they were not rich, nor to my knowledge, did they ever become so. The child was called the son of God - so why the need for another? And why was it necessary for the child Carol was allegedly carrying to be favoured with the very best money can buy?

Come the evening when the requested pools coupon was placed on the table with the twenty-six letters and *yes* and *no*. There was a conversation between God and ourselves prior to the anticipated team selection, concerning what, I cannot recall, but I had these questions demanding to be answered before the team choice business could begin. I could hold them back no longer.

"Where does Jesus Christ fit into all this"? I blurted out, "He was born in a stable and did not need lots of money."

The glass went absolutely berserk . It tore round the table at break-neck speed spelling out, *JESUS CHRIST IS A LOST SOUL*. I have no recollection of any further conversation with the god of the glass, but indelibly printed on my memory is the terrible anger my question had provoked.

The outcome was that the glass would no longer work for us, God was now refusing to talk to us through it. We placed our fingers on it many times, pleading with it to respond, but it was as if it were superglued. We were now in a terrifying limbo, the voice of God we had been so carefully trained to recognise had not gone away and was becoming inextricably intermingled with our own thought processes. This was the beginning of a very real fear campaign, conflicting words were injected into our already confused minds, driving us towards insanity.

To be in a strait between two mental processes, not knowing our own thoughts from those being thrust into us, together with the very real possibility of further offending an already offended God, was like living in a surreal nightmare. Yet knowing always that you were wide awake and the circumstances would not go away.

Lewd and crude thoughts incessantly found their way in, the urge to speak foul language constantly had to be held back, obscenities seemed to be everywhere, and there was no refuge from them. I envied everyone else, they were not living this nightmare, they had normal lives. Carol meanwhile was experiencing mental torments similar to mine. Our bad dreams were increasing in intensity. Many night hours were spent praying and pleading for each other and our two girls, our short period of sleep provided little respite from our awful circumstance.

Our two daughters, the house, our appearance, everything was being neglected, so wrapped up were we with our involvement with the god of the glass. It was not only myself that was lost and destined for hell, but as the proposed son was no longer relevant, Carol was now under the same condemnation.

Somewhere in the house there was a Bible, maybe if I could find it and read it, God might speak to us through it. Apparently, it is not a good idea to open a Bible at random and expect to read what you want to read, but I knew nothing of that.

After a bit of a rummage I found it and opened it up randomly. It fell open at Job 23, and I read, *even today is my complaint bitter, my stroke is heavier than my groaning, oh that I might know where I might find him and that I might come even to his seat, I would order my cause before him fill my mouth with arguments. I would know the words which he would answer me and understand what he would say to me.*

Verse 8 goes on to say, *behold I go forward, but he is not there; and backward but I cannot perceive him, on the left hand where he doth work, but I cannot behold him, he hides himself on the right that I cannot see him. (KJV)*

All so incredibly uncannily relevant, yet I found no comfort in those words, they spoke only of my desperate search to establish contact with God. If I had taken notice of what verse 10 says, *but he knows the way that I take, when he has tried me, I shall come forth as gold. (KJV)* I may have glimpsed some light, but I was too deep into wretchedness and misery to accommodate uplifting thoughts. We could no longer go on like this; something had to be done, but what?

Carol and I discussed it and realised that ours was a problem that no medical practitioner could deal with. What if we went to church? God's house. That might help.

The following Sunday morning as we had resolved, we went to a Church. I am unable to remember anything about the service because for the entire time we could only feel the cold draught of God's presence. Going to that church offered no cure for our dilemma. The night of 13th February 1969 was so dreadful that we had no option other than to speak to a minister of the church.

Next morning, without an appointment, we knocked on the manse door of the local Methodist minister, Rev Allan Fisher answered and said he had someone with him, and would we mind waiting a while? As we sat in our van, Carol said, "let's go, I don't think there is any point speaking to him." But I insisted we go through with it. A couple of eternities later, the manse door opened, someone came out and Rev' Fisher beckoned us in.

For two hours we opened up, during which Mary, his wife, who had been out came into the room, and they both just listened. Mary was so amazed that she burned her fish fingers to a cinder

I had to terminate the visit at 1.30pm as I was due on shift at 2.00pm. Rev Fisher said a brief word of prayer before we left and promised Carol he would call in to see her later that afternoon. I arrived late for work to find a problem had occurred that morning that was my job to sort out. This was the straw that broke the camel's back. my tormented brain went into overdrive; so much time had gone by and I still had not sorted the problem. A few nights earlier, I had a dream I was in a very tall building where someone was telling me to pull myself together.

At work my foreman found me wandering around where tanks of chemicals are stored, and, yes, he told me to pull myself together. He also told me to report to the nurse. It was already around 8pm. She assessed my condition and somehow arranged a doctor's appointment for the next morning, Saturday.

Arriving home, I found Carol more at ease, Rev Fisher had visited her as promised and that had helped greatly, but for me things were far from good. I really needed to go to the manse, in that house there was a peace that was tangible. As I sat in their living room, I felt something of normality returning and the calm that radiated from the Rev and Mary spoke to me of a possibility that there may yet be a way out of our situation.

The telephone rang, it was Carol phoning from a neighbour's house as we did not have a phone. "She wants you home right away," said Rev' Fisher, "she sounds very frightened. I will follow on after you."

How things had changed. Only 52 days previously I was a confirmed atheist always ready to ridicule the Church, and now it seems our only real hope of escaping from this nightmare could be through a minister of the Church. Though how he could bring it about, I did not have a clue. I found Carol in an agitated condition. She was experiencing an intense cold presence in the room and was afraid the *god* that controlled the glass would appear. Rev Fisher arrived a few minutes after me.

We sat down and he explained the true nature of God, how He loved us so much that He gave His only son, Jesus Christ, to die in our place, a substitute sacrifice for our sin, and that through Him we have a way back to God. He spoke of the god of the glass, and said that he was not able to say before as it could have added to our confused condition, but he who claimed to be God was really a spirit the Bible calls the devil.

I was not completely naïve, and had begun to doubt for some time that the regime of fear imposed on Carol and myself was compatible with any God I had heard of. Things were getting a little clearer, but how could our release come about? Would God, the *real* God ever forgive people like us?

Rev Fisher told us of a painting by Holman Hunt, a picture of Jesus standing at a door with no handle on the outside. He pointed us to a verse in Revelation 3-20 that says *behold I stand at the door and knock, if any man hears my voice and opens the door I will come in and sup with him.* kjv Rev Fisher then told us that the door represents the door of our hearts, and if we want Jesus to come in and save us, the handle is on the inside. We ourselves have to open it; He will not push His way into our lives.

We knelt down and prayed as Rev Fisher directed, confessing to God our sinful condition and claiming forgiveness in Jesus name, asking Him to come into our lives

It seemed such a simple thing to do, but the peace and calmness of mind that immediately embraced us both, was undeniable. We had no real understanding of the miracle transaction that had taken place, but we did know that we enjoyed a peaceful night's sleep, the first for many weeks.

The next morning, I attended my doctor's appointment, and was amazed that he already knew so much about me, the nurse had obviously briefed him, I felt the consultation went well, however, the doctor was not impressed. He prescribed sedatives and made a further appointment for the following Monday morning. It seems he also contacted Rev and Mary Fisher to see if they were able to help me (Mary was a district nurse working out of the practise) otherwise he was going to have to refer me for psychiatric treatment.

Later that day, Rev' Fisher collected me from home and took me to tax my van, but the post office was closed. On the way home he called in at a local hospital to visit a member of his congregation, asking if I would mind waiting a while. As I sat in his car, I heard that familiar voice saying, "do you really believe God will forgive you?"

On his return, Rev Fisher said "he had just been talking to a woman who is very near to death, and she knows it. She had told him there were many things she does not understand about spiritual matters but soon she would be with the One who would provide all the answers. I doubt that I will ever know how that impacted my thought processes, but by the time we had travelled the few miles to our house, it seemed as if a dark cloud had been lifted from my mind. I left the car and floated into the house with the euphoria of the newly liberated, I was lost in that unrepeatable moment so perceptively penned by Charles Wesley.

Long my imprisoned spirit lay,
fast bound in sin and natures night.
Thine eye diffused a quickening ray,
I woke the dungeon flamed with light,
My chains fell off, my heart was free,
I rose went forth and followed thee.

Seeing my face in a mirror eventually brought me down to Earth, I was grey-faced and gaunt, my eyes red, rimmed and bloodshot from so many sleepless nights pleading for help from the imposter god. My lips were dry and sore, I had been biting them raw. I went out and bought some lip salve and eye ointment. I had a new determination and resolve that on my Monday visit to the doctor, not only my appearance but my whole demeanour would be changed; I would also return the sedatives unopened as I would have no need of them.

Later that day, Carol, the girls and I were returning from a visit to my parents when we stopped walking and looked at each other. At the same instant we both heard the familiar voice say, "so you think you have escaped." We agreed that we needed to make a meaningful and practical act of total separation from that which had nearly wrecked our lives. I do not know what our neighbours must have thought, but when we arrived home, we went through all our cupboards and smashed every wine glass we might have used in conversations with the spirit who called himself *god*.

On the Monday I returned the sedatives to the doctor unopened, and he was satisfied that I needed no further consultations. In retrospect, I find this rather odd, one and a half days earlier he was contemplating having me sectioned for psychiatric treatment with the possibility of the girls being taken from us for a while, yet he found me perfectly sound. Had he witnessed something of the miraculous?

Every aspect of our lives from that weekend on was radically changed. We found ourselves involved in so many church activities, our house became a magnet for many local teenagers. There were Bible studies, outreach works, Sunday school teaching and visits to hospitals and elderly people's homes. We just loved it.

Many people shared stories of encounters with the *moving glass*, particularly the young. To some it was frightening, but to the majority it was nothing other than an amusing pastime. Most have no interest in understanding the power that enables the glass to move, ask and answer questions intelligently. For myself, having been deceived and tormented by this invisible force that demonstrated its ability to communicate through a clear manufactured inanimate object, was a puzzle I needed to investigate further. It would be remiss of me, having stimulated a curiosity in some to understand more of this enigmatic force, to leave our story here.

CHAPTER NINE
So Who? The Devil, is it?

God is spirit, we are part spirit, made in his image. My tormentor was spirit. There is a dearth of belief in the existence of a spiritual dimension, and as it is my desire in these pages to awaken our conception to the frailty of evolutionary evidences, so I also feel I need to include my experiential assessment of the glass-moving power that it might awaken in some an awareness of the reality of spirituality.

I am convinced that the *Nan Bennet* character and subsequent god personality was one and the same. The first was an introductory easing into our confidence by the deceitful assuming of being a well-loved family member. *God is listening*, was a further clever ploy to prepare us for the god character, which in itself was another assumed title hiding the true identity of our contact.

This invisible force asks and answers questions, considers circumstances, deceives, dominates, employs mind games, and is, because of his advantages, more than a match for our flesh-bound intelligence. His power is not contained within the glass. Indeed, the manufactured Ouija board does not employ a glass as such, the alphabet circle and *Yes* and *No* hold no mystic power, they are all simply means of communication.

So, what does move the glass? Is there some hitherto untapped power in human minds allied to the bodies electrical energies that motivates it, thus in some way making the players the activators? That being the case, why should Carol and I be transmitting thoughts detrimental to us?

And why when we so desperately wanted it to move to answer our mind confusing questions, it refused to do so?

If it were that the glass moved in relation to our own thought patterns, it would surely have reacted in accordance with our dual inconsolable desires. It could be some form of influence, someone suggested to me, what exactly did they mean by that I ask myself; it had shown itself to have intelligence, therefore it is an intelligent influence, and a free thinking clever influence must emanate from a life form of some sort, albeit spiritual.

Some think the glass moves in some way by static electricity, possibly as it moves along a surface? Therefore, it would need a charge to get it moving in the first instance, it would also need to be linked to the intelligence it displayed, and be inseparable from it. The old accusation that someone is pushing it falls at the first hurdle, as Carol and I have known it moving without our fingers on it as it was moving so fast we were unable to keep up, others have witnessed this too, could it be that the dead can be contacted through the various spiritual methods?

Carol's grandmother, Nan Bennett, was supposedly now in Heaven. Was it actually her that we were speaking to? If so, how is it that the god that was with her and subsequently took over the conversation, showed himself to be a liar, deceiver and a purveyor of fear, with a strong aversion to the name of Jesus Christ? Would the God of Heaven be so abusive to His own son? Remember what he said when I questioned him about that name? *Jesus Christ is a lost soul.* The pseudo-god most certainly was not speaking from Heaven.

The Bible says, those who claim to be able to speak to the dead are an abomination to God.

When you enter the land the Lord your God is giving you, do not learn to imitate the detestable ways of the nations there. Let no one be found among you who sacrifices their son or daughter in the fire, who practices divination or sorcery, interprets omens, engages in witchcraft, or casts spells, or who is a medium or spiritist or who consults the dead. Anyone who does these things is detestable to the Lord;...
(Deuteronomy 18:9-12)

The true nature of the personality we invite into our lives is, to those who have done it, totally unknown, yet out of blind curiosity we foolishly continue. It ingratiates itself into our confidence with its initially relaxed familiarity. He has the ability to infiltrate our minds, he deliberately taught Carol and me to listen for and recognise his *voice*, a weapon later used against us to great advantage. When refusing to activate the glass during our last two-way conversation, he knowingly left us in a dangerously unstable situation and had it not been that we were led (as I believe we were) to a couple that recognised the problem and knew the only solution, our story to date would have been so very different. Psychiatric remedies had no chance of digging out the root of it, the drugs may have stabilised us, and so calloused over it, thus turning us, over the years, into burned out schizophrenics.

It is an obvious conclusion, you may think, for Bible believers to consider this alien force to be the devil. To most people he is a pantomime figure, usually in red tights with horns on his head, always playfully tempting us to do wrong. He inhabits some fiery place of torture or carnal pleasure where deviants go when they die. In reality, Satan is not in the least bit amusing or virtuous. He delights to be misunderstood and purposely propagates this false image of himself, so unbelievable, so laughable, that he furthers his objective of denying his own existence.

So, what does the Bible say about him that points to him as the number one suspect, not only as the invisible power behind the mystery of the moving glass, but of many other well documented phenomena? Many folk-law misconceptions have evolved over the years, giving this character his mythological status.

Most people speak of him as *the devil*, singular, but in the Scriptures, Jesus often speaks of *devils*. John in the book of Revelation, records that Satan was cast out of Heaven and his angels with him, (Revelation 12:9) He called himself *God*, and indeed, this Satan or Lucifer, had desires to be equal with God.

In 2 Corinthians 4:3-4 Paul writes of him as the god *of this world*, he is referred to as *the prince of this world*, and as *the prince of the power of the air* in Ephesians 2:2 he operates within a dimension that our finite minds are totally unable to comprehend, almost as if he and his followers inhabit our atmosphere. These are the devils, the demons, which Carol and I unfortunately contacted that Boxing Day afternoon. The world for the most part is oblivious of it, but there is a mighty battle going on for the minds of all of us.

How, you may well ask, can spirits pretending to be our dead loved ones and speaking through a glass or a medium, turn people's mind away from spiritual things? Surely the opposite is the case. The answer is simple, every allegedly dead person contacted in this manner, is found to be in a good place, usually Heaven. They may speak of problems left behind but all are in some form of paradise. In this clever deception, the death of Jesus on the cross is not needed, If we all go to heaven there is no judgment to face, therefore no substitute sacrifice is required. An environment of false security is propagated and the need for repentance becomes null and void.

People enthuse about the possibility of life on other planets, when living here invisibly among us, is this spiritual life form whose sole purpose is to wreck and destroy; not only individual lives, but the entire fabric of society that God intended for mankind – the work He began in the garden of Eden. The *aliens* are here already. And so certain are they that they have blinded our eyes to their existence that they can openly toy with us. They are more than adequately equipped to deceive both individuals and nations.

Paul in his letter to the church at Ephesus writes *that we wrestle not against flesh and blood, but against principalities, against powers, against the rulers of the darkness of this world, against spiritual wickedness in high places.* (Ephesians 6:12 KJV)

These spirits are the male voice coming from the female medium, the information provider for the past-life *regressionist*, the mover of objects we call poltergeist, the apparition we call ghost, the occult power of the witchdoctor, the intelligence behind the Ouija board and so much more. The complexity and diversity of devices used to deny or misrepresent our understanding that God is, are truly awesome, and top of the list is *atheism* camouflaged as evolution. Seemingly scientific and so innocent, yet it deprives millions of their birthright to a faith in God by its lawful dominance.

Even in the West we have adopted an acceptance of certain activities. Witchcraft and even Satanism is today considered benign; *It doesn't affect me so Let them get on with it, no harm done.* The *intelligence* that asked and answered our questions would have no problem deceiving a receptive audience, eager to communicate with deceased loved ones. The voice that infiltrated our minds so easily has unlimited scope for wickedness on an unthinkable scale.

Why did this enigmatic intelligence display such anger, shout abuse about Jesus, then run and hide refusing to be contacted through the glass again? At that time, he had us both in the palm of his hand. The simple answer is that he was afraid. The very name of Jesus strikes fear into unclean spirits, and in this reaction, he inadvertently revealed who he is, a spirit of anti-Christ. There is a Scripture, 1 John 3:8, that states the reason the son of God appeared was to destroy the devil's work. They know Him and are justifiably afraid of Him.

Mathew, Mark and Luke relate many instances of Jesus casting out and rebuking devils. His power over such is unquestionable, and they are aware that they are running out of time. He is the reason that even saying the name of Jesus caused our tormenter to run. The existence and activities of these spirits are by no means confined to the lifetime of Jesus. I have no doubt whatsoever if I put out a request on the Internet for stories of demonic involvement in people's lives, I would receive many up–to-date stories, identifiably different to psychological malady.

The son that Carol and myself were told was needed to be born into the world was more than a deceit perpetrated on two gullible individuals, it has a biblical parallel. There is fast approaching a day indelibly written into Scripture, when this satanic spirit will be seen embodied in a man.

I am convinced that the mover of the glass is none other than a demonic spirit. They alone are the correct shape to fit into the universal jigsaw puzzle, and if indeed the devil has shown himself to be a reality and the biblical account of him is true, then it obviously follows on that God is, and so is his son, Jesus Christ.

The Bible tells us that God made us in His image and this can be seen in many ways, but there is an important truth here that Satan has seen fit to attack in order to dilute. God is in three persons: Father, Son and Holy

Spirit, so likewise, he made us: body, soul and spirit, It is the part of us that cannot die that is so neglected, the spirit. It is so important for us to understand this, in order to understand ourselves as complete human beings. We are not a species.

The Scriptures are in no way unclear about this. When Paul was signing off his letter to the Christians at Thessalonica, he said, *I pray God your whole spirit, soul and body be preserved..* (1 Thessalonians 5:23) When Mary, the mother of Jesus, was rejoicing with Elizabeth, the mother of John the Baptist about her pregnancy, she said, *my soul glorifies the Lord and my spirit rejoices in God my Saviour.* (Luke 1:46) When Stephen was being stoned he called out to God, *to receive my spirit.* (Acts 7:59) In his first letter to the church at Corinth, Paul posed the question, *what man knows the things of man save the spirit of man which is in him?* (1 Corinthians 2:11) Later he encourages them to, *Glorify God in their bodies and in their spirits, which are God's.* (1 Corinthians 6:20) Finally, a quote from the Old Testament, Ecclesiastes 3:20, *and the dust returns to the ground it came from. and the spirit returns to God who gave it.* There are many, many more.

Like it or not, believe it or not, we are more than just flesh and blood. At creation we were all given a spirit and that spirit, cannot die. Where that spirit spends eternity is entirely in our own hands. The most fear-filled facet of my involvement with the *god of the glass* was to be told that I was irretrievably lost to an eternity in Hell.

I now know this was a false god, an imposter, but I am also now aware that Almighty God, the maker and creator of all things, is the God of light, of love and truth, and that all good things emanate from Him. To step out into an eternity that is without light and loveless, having been told by the Lord Himself, *go away I never knew you,* would be a fate too dreadful to contemplate. I do not know what Hell is, it could be a condition or a place, but of this I am sure, if it is an eternal separation from the very source of all light and life, with no hope of reconciliation, then we, all of us, need urgently to do whatever it takes to avoid that condemnation.

I know this is not an acceptable subject, but having tapped into that evil spiritual force, and having had an experiential awareness of the reality of the existence of a spiritual dimension, I feel that it falls heavily on me to make others aware of these truths.

It is extremely unlikely that many will ever become entangled in the sort of traumatic spiritual net that ensnared Carol and myself, but invisibly, inaudibly and imperceptibly, the battle for every human spirit continues. I am in no doubt whatsoever that there is a heaven to gain and a hell to shun, and the choice of your eternal habitation, is yours and yours alone. Frankly, if someone had come to me in the days of my atheism with a story such as ours, I would have been looking over their shoulders for the men in white coats. It *was made easy for you to believe,* someone once said, but I can assure you, being saved from the edge of insanity was not easy.

Fifty-two days were all that were needed to turn an ordinary young couple, innocently dabbling in that which they failed to recognise as the occult, into that which confronted Alan and Mary Fisher on 14th February 1969. Yes, I am now eighty four- and Carol went to be with the Lord in October 2018, and although the things that took place are now more than half a lifetime away, I still recall them as though it were yesterday.

When our spiritual encounter first became known, there was some publicity given to it based on an outline of our experience; a spread in a Christian newspaper, a brief chapter in a book, a flyer on the dangers of involvement with the occult, and later an interview on Christan TV. But I still felt the need to put together a fuller account.

Spiritualism in its various forms is increasingly gripping the minds of many today with its mysterious magnetism. I hope that the reading of this testimony and analysis of the evil forces behind them, will break bondages and draw people into a relationship with the one true God through His son Jesus Christ. Jesus, in our darkest hour, rescued us, has kept us, and will keep us in a sure and certain knowledge that one day we will meet Him face to face.

For he has rescued us from the dominion of darkness and brought us into the kingdom of the son he loves. In whom we have redemption the forgiveness of sins. (Colossians 1:13-14) It is impossible for me not to believe God, or indeed the world of the spirit.

Millions of folks go about their daily lives oblivious to the consequence of their rejection of God. That is why this next section needs to be included; in order to give a full understanding of what it is all about.

CHAPTER TEN
Pear-shaped in a Garden

For many years the idea has been propagated that scientific progress and good education, together with sensible diet and adequate sanitation will provide the answers to all man's ills; and where are we today? Struggling with a plethora of economic difficulties, assaulted by crime at its most basic and violent type, to the ingenious and sophisticated scams that blight all societies, corporate and individual greed, corruption up to governmental levels, blatant sexual immorality and perversion, etc. It often appears that the whole fabric of our society is degenerating, and increasingly so with each new generation. It is generally seen as progress .Could it be that we have set sail from the haven of status-quo, and jettisoned the compass?

There are so many personal and international tragedies we hear of that cause both believers and unbelievers to cry out, why does God allow it to happen? If God is love, how can He just sit back looking at all the misery in the world and do nothing about it?

This question must rank top of the list of those asked of God by all mankind: Without any understanding of the bigger picture, it is a justifiable stumbling block to belief in Him. The story of Adam and Eve is another that over the years has attracted much ridicule, but along with the story of Noah it carries a very important message for us all.

The key to our understanding almost all the questions we may ever pose concerning our relationship to God and His to us, is to be found in that which took place in the garden of Eden, as this is where it all went *pear-shaped*.

There were only two newly created people in that garden; a man and a woman. Their every need was catered for and they had an intimate relationship with their God who had created them in His own image, and had breathed the life of the spirit into them. They had eternal life; they should not have to die. It must have been an incredibly beautiful place, and it was all theirs to enjoy. There was only one rule that God had given them. There would have been many trees in that garden, but God told them not to eat of the tree in the middle, because they would surely die. (Genesis 2:15-17) There is an urge endemic in us all, that when told not to do something, the drive is so powerful that we just do it. But the penalty for disobeying God's command was very severe.

The narrative goes on to tell us of a third party in the garden with them; it had the form of a serpent and was able to converse with Eve. Let us pause a moment and look at a portion of Scripture that puts this being into perspective.

Revelation 12:7-9, ... *and there was war in heaven: Michael and his Angels fought against the dragon; and the dragon and his angels fought back but he was not strong enough. And they lost their place in heaven, the great dragon was hurled down-that ancient serpent, called the devil, or Satan, who leads the whole world astray, he was hurled to Earth and his angels with him.*

Let us examine how he goes about his first deception of humanity as read in Genesis 3. *"Did God really say you must not eat from any tree in the garden?"* he asked Eve. This first question is designed to sow doubt in her mind, but the woman replied, *"we may eat fruit from the trees in the garden but God did say, you must not eat fruit from the tree in the middle of the garden, and you must not touch it or you will die."*

The next words of the serpent speak in direct opposition to the instructions given by God: *You shall surely not die, for God knows that when you eat of it your eyes will be opened and you will be like God knowing good and evil.* Satan is hinting here that God is concealing something from them that will put them on a level footing with Him. At that moment both the man and woman were innocent, and that which Satan told her was partially true, they would come to know good and evil, though, unknown to her, that would be disastrously detrimental to them both, and in the contemplation of that gain, Eve lost sight of the promise that in partaking of the fruit of that tree, she would surely die.

Eve chose to believe the devil's lies, and rejected the truth given to her by her creator, the bottom line being that she saw the serpent's arguments as being more acceptable to her than God's, and in doing so, declared Him to be a liar. Adam went along with this, he did not rebuke her for disbelieving their creator, but instead ate the fruit she gave him.

Many believe this story to be purely symbolic, however, the genealogy of Jesus in Luke's Gospel reads back to Adam, so surely this unbroken continuity is an evidence that Adam and Eve were flesh and blood, the first of humanity to live on Earth. Do you recognise today's society in the story so far? God's truth is discarded out of hand and replaced with lies, deceit and disbelief. We prefer our own understanding: who needs God? Can His word really be relied on? Anyway we evolved, science has proved it, there is no God...

This most ancient of all stories has so much to say about our contemporary situation and it contains within it an answer to that most asked of questions, why does God allow it to happen?

There was another very important tree in the garden and its fruit could be taken and eaten by the duo at any time. One tree led to death, the other led to life. Given such a choice, would you not choose the one that led to life? Or would you? Millennia have passed since Adam and Eve made the wrong choice, now each one of us has the same offer available: a literal life or death decision. It is so sad that so many still make the wrong choice.

The single law Adam and Eve had broken carried with it the same inevitability as a jump from the world's tallest building, *if you do this you will surely die*. He who designed the universe and all that is in it, is no stranger to extrapolation. God recognised from that one dismissal of His truth, law and authority, the inevitable increase of sin with each succeeding generation. For evidence we only need consider standards in our own lifetimes.

God had to drive the pair out of the garden because the tree of life and the entrance into His eternity was there, and if they had been able to gain access to it after their blatant disobedience, out of control corruption would inevitably permeate both heaven and Earth. The serpent and his fallen angel followers would continue to have power and influence over Adam and Eve's descendants as indeed they do have on Earth to this day).

We read in Genesis 3:24, that after God had driven the man out, He placed on the east side of the garden, cherubim and a flaming sword, flashing back and forth to guard the tree of life. Irrespective of what we consider the cherubim and flaming sword to be, there is no question that of our own volition, no one will ever find the entrance into eternal life. Our ever increasing knowledge may extend our Earth lives, but eternity is God's prerogative

God's foresight was made clear within a few generations of the exit from the garden. Cain, Adam's first-born son, murdered his brother, Abel, and so the degeneration escalated until, by the time of Noah, we read in Genesis 6:5-7, *and God saw how great man's wickedness on Earth had become, and that Every inclination of the thoughts his heart was only evil all the time.* It had taken only ten generations for humanity to become so retrograde.

Here lies the answer to our age-old question, why does God allow it to happen? It lies firmly at our own feet. Our forebears set God's advice at naught and preferred their own understanding. Is it not so today? So, out of the garden they had to go, from thereon in dependent upon their own abilities, inventiveness, moral judgment, governments etc. We were now the masters of our planet and all that is in it including its multiple resources and inherent unpredictability.

The theme song of man must surely be, *I did it my way*, and as we do it our way, we encounter overwhelming problems, often coming about as a result of our own actions, and yet we send up the usual question to God.

Earth and all that is in it, is governed by unchangeable physical laws. It is ageing and we are powerless to intervene over so many things. There are tectonic plates colliding, volcanoes erupting, resources diminishing, populations increasing, social economic systems failing, weather patterns changing, waters, land and air needlessly being polluted, inherited genetic disorders increasing, while faith in the One who has ultimate control, is rejected out of hand at both personal and international level.

Those who would point to God and His providence are progressively marginalised. To blame and question God is in the least, unfair. From the moment of the fall, He conceived a plan to rescue us. We can read about it being worked out throughout the Scriptures, through Noah, Abraham, Jacob, (who became Israel), Joseph, Moses, David, the nation of Israel and so many others who played a pivotal role In God's restoration plan for us all, culminating in Jesus Christ and His work on the cross.

Paul's first letter to the Corinthians tells it exactly as it is, *for since death, came through a man, the resurrection of the dead comes also, through a man, for as in Adam all die, so, in Christ all will be made alive.* (1 Corinthians 15:21-22) Adam died because of his disobedience to God, Jesus died in obedience and so was resurrected into eternal life, and *even so in Christ shall all be made alive.* It is an incredible mystery, but one that once embraced, has a wonderful way of changing lives.

For it to all go pear-shaped in Eden must have taken only a few moments, to put things right is taking God millennia, but immediately after things went wrong, God foreshadowed His ultimate intention. He Himself provided animal skins to clothe the naked pair, a precursor to Jesus' righteousness eventually being available to cover our sinfulness. I will never cease to be amazed at the immaculate continuity of the Scriptures from cover to cover.

CHAPTER ELEVEN
The Ultimate Crucible

There has to be a reason for all this, the unique Earth, the universe, the fall of man, reconciliation through Jesus and so much more. What is it all about? Is there any meaning or purpose to our existence?

Before we approach the subject, we need to remind ourselves that all we can perceive and understand with our natural physical senses is not all that there is. To make the claim, as I am doing, that the invisible God is the author and creator of all things, is in direct opposition to the mass acceptance of the evolutionary theory, and would be incomplete without an investigation into the reason for it all. The sciences have no explanation other than that we are a miniscule product of an explosion of particle interaction billions of years ago, during which, through a process equivalent to a lottery, all things came into being as we now see them. There is no purpose in this philosophy, and our fleeting involvement in it. As just another species, ours is to live, die and be as if we had never been.

In contrast; that which I place before you now, has a beginning, a middle and an end. It is a concept that takes us out of the realms of earthly understanding, into the spiritual dimension, where we have a glimpse of circumstances from God's perspective and a purpose, culminating in a glorious everlasting finality.

There are two outstanding facets of the nature of God to be found in the Bible. One is His unfathomable love, the other is that He will not tolerate sin, and by that, not just the things we recognise as sinful. Disobedience to His will is unacceptable to God, so when we read of a rebellion taking place in heaven, no way will it be taken lightly.

The Bible talks of Angels, Seraphim and Cherubim, and others of which we do not have any real understanding, other than that they may have been created by God to serve him in various ways. Most of us would have recited some time, "thy will be done on Earth as it is in heaven", and so it is without question at all times. It is difficult for us to understand from our earthbound situation that in a different dimension beyond our comprehension, events have taken place that have a direct effect upon our lives both here on Earth and on into eternity.

There is no way God would allow a rebellion and disobedience in heaven to Continue. The Scriptures giving the account of that rebellion are found in Revelation 12:7-8, telling of the battle with Michael and his angels defeating Satan and casting him out of heaven to Earth. We looked at this Scripture in the previous chapter but I will quote verse 12 again because of its relevance to the text. *Therefore, rejoice you heavens, and you that dwell in them. But woe to the Earth and the sea . Because the devil has gone down to you, he is filled with fury, because he knows that his time is short.*

All of these fallen Angels are eternal beings, they cannot die, so where does God go from here?

God created man out of a deep desire to share His eternity with those who will love Him for His own sake, of their own free will. We read many times in the Bible of the praise and worship given to Him by His created subjects in heaven, but He desires the love of those who having not seen Him, have believed that He (this is important) is their creator.

We are given no concise details of either times or the sequence of events, especially when we move into the last days as recorded in Revelation. *In the beginning God created the heavens and the Earth..."* It was not a whim He could do it, so He did; no, it was created for a purpose, and this is where our lack of understanding of God's timing becomes blurred.

Without doubt, Earth was formed as a dwelling place for man, all of its uniqueness, beauty and perfection are for us. We may never know of God's ultimate plans for us, but into this perfection came Satan and his fellow fallen angels, and everything changed. Satan had by his desires to be equal with God, brought sin into heaven and now had begun to permeate mankind with his sin, he was now as Scripture describes him, *the prince and the god of this world.*(John 16:11)

So, I repeat the question, where does God go from here? How does one deal with the problem of impurity? You pass it through a process of purification.

The rebellion of Satan and the angels he had taken along with him, presented God with the same circumstance He confronted in the Garden of Eden, the rejection of His authority. Although God Himself is pure and holy, He is aware of the potential for evil that exists within His creation, and will not permit its perpetrators into His presence. This problem of endemic sin had to be eradicated, it had infected a section of His angelic host, and He knew it would spoil the lives of those with whom He intended to share His eternity.

When a craftsman in precious metals purifies them, he places them in a vessel called a crucible, he then applies heat sufficient to melt it. In that process the impurities or *dross* rises to the surface, this is then discarded. He will carry out this process of heating and throwing away the dross until he obtains the level of purity he requires.

This Earth that God created is now the ultimate crucible, designed and crafted for the benefit of mankind. Yes, though now its primary purpose is as the vessel whereby He is able to carry out His refining process, the preparation of a people who would love Him and serve Him unconditionally.

And the fallen angels? They are here on Earth unseen, even denying their own existence yet playing a part in the refining of God's people. That is crazy you say, fallen angels that had directly opposed God's will now used by Him in the purification of His elect? In this we again see the amazing intellect of God. Into this earthly crucible He places the whole of humanity, together with all the problems and temptations the world can hurl at them, with the additional exacerbations those spirits of anti-Christ can so easily throw into that purifying vessel.

This is how it is with God's refining process, many and varied are the circumstances He employs as He skims away the earthiness of the natures of those He is transforming into the image of His son, Jesus, the express image of His being. These thoughts are brought into perspective when set against Peter's writing in his first Epistle.

Praise be to the God, and Father of our Lord Jesus Christ . in His great mercy he has given us new birth into a living hope through the resurrection of Jesus Christ from the dead, and into an inheritance that can never perish, spoil or fade, kept in heaven for you who through faith are shielded by God's power until the coming of the salvation that is ready to be revealed in the last time. In this you greatly rejoice, though for a season you may have had to suffer grief in all kinds of trial's, these have come so that your faith of far greater worth than gold, which perishes even though refined by fire, may prove genuine, and may result in praise, glory and honor when Jesus Christ is revealed. (1 Peter 1:3-7)

God is in the process of separating and refining a people to share His eternity, but how does this help in dealing with the problem of the angels that rebelled against His authority? They are spiritual beings and they cannot die. There is a Scripture that says, *do you not know that you will judge angels?* (1 Corinthians 6:3) It is referring to those angels that left their first estate; they also will face a day of reckoning in some way related to their opposition to God's restoration work here on Earth.

Their eternal fate is too dreadful to contemplate. We can read of it towards the end of the book of Revelation, yet another long reading. But having considered Satan's works, it is correct that we should be aware of his end.

And I saw an angel come down from heaven, having the key of the Abyss and holding in his hand a great chain. He seized the dragon. That ancient serpent, who is the devil, or Satan, and bound him for a thousand years. He threw him into the Abyss, and locked and sealed it over him, to keep him from deceiving the nations any more until the thousand years were ended. after that he must be set free for a short time.(Revelation 20:1-3)

Jesus Christ will reign on Earth during those thousand years, That period on Earth will be so different; *the wolf and the lamb shall feed together,* is the Bible's perfect summery of it. (Isaiah 65:25) But there will be those not content with things as they are, and a further purification is called for. Many generations will enter the world during those thousand years and all will not appreciate the quality of life under King Jesus.

In verse 7 we read, *when the thousand years are over, Satan shall be released from his prison",* and part of verse 8, *"and will go out to deceive the nations.* He was involved in gathering them together for the final battle, which they had no hope of winning, and we read that fire came down from heaven and devoured them.

Verse 10: *and the devil who deceived them was thrown into the lake of burning Sulphur where the beast and the false prophet had been thrown. They will be tormented day and night forever and ever.*

Without doubt, I have strayed from my earlier considerations of the frailty of the evolutionist argument when compared to the unquestionable accuracy of scriptural prophesy, yet in a way that is not entirely true. The more we understand of the whole council of God, the more we appreciate its authenticity. It embraces the whole of human life and beyond into eternity, holding out a place in that eternal life for those who put their trust in God. Evolution, on the other hand, offers an unproveable theory paraded as proven fact, which when embraced, guarantees that death is the end of us. We are, according to their doctrine, just another species, nothing more.

I mentioned previously that Christianity has a beginning, a middle and an end. We shall consider the end at the end. If you are adamant that all things came together by chance, it is worth considering that both logic and common sense tell us that no amount of thought can change us into another physical form. In order to strive in some way or other towards some envisaged, more attractive or better equipped for purpose being, would necessitate a knowledge of that which you wished to be; a preconceived self-design. This concept of yours would then need to be passed on through succeeding generations. This raises the insurmountable problem of how to set about achieving it.

Chance mutations? They are inevitably a fault and impossible to control, and if progression towards perfection takes place through chance fortuitous mutations, why is it that every living thing on the planet, stands today perfectly formed? Not one single entity can be seen in a transitory state, and despite verbal and graphic manipulations, neither can it be said of fossilised forms.

Jesus in His sermon on the mount (and He should know what He is talking about) asks, *who of you by worrying can add a single cubit to his height?* (Matthew 6:27)

The mathematical probability of just one living thing being formed to its present state of perfection through the process of evolution is beyond comprehension: every bird, fish, animal, insect, and man is perfectly designed for its purpose within a carefully conceived inter-related world order. Add each one together with all the others and the colossal number of zeros would confirm the improbability of perfection through a method, that has so much in common with a lottery.

The old monkey and typewriter illustration puts it all in perspective.

For a monkey to type *p* followed by an *e* is a probability of 1 in 3600.

For a monkey to type *peanut* the chance decreases to 1 in 46,656,000,000.

For a monkey to type *monkey and typewriters*, (23 letters with spaces) it would take one million monkeys over one thousand, million, million, million, million years at three letters per second. Just to achieve those two words.

Mathematicians agree that any requisite number beyond 10 to the power of 50 (that is 10 followed by 50 zeros) has statistically a zero possibility of occurrence. There is a tendency to confuse adaption with evolution, built into all living things is the abiiity to adapt to circumstance, yet all remain within their kind, interbreeding restricted by their genetic structure, as in Genesis 1.

Numerous times in documentaries we hear that this creature developed a particular facet of its being; *how?* In making such comments these people are stepping outside of the realms of common sense, it is almost too ridiculous to analyse. First it would have to consider the change it desired: to improve its colour, its shape, its function, etc. Sounds easy if you say it fast, but the technicalities involved in even one single change to a creature's form or appearance would be extremely complex, and that is not even considering the essential rearranging of its DNA profile.

Then, through some magical process, the original individual would need to pass on their perceived design to the products of their procreation over, it would seem, many millions of years hoping to achieve this through the lottery of fortuitous mutations. Intelligent people are making these statements, so either they have not considered the implications of their comments, or it is deceit.

Forgive me for applying a very silly illustration, but it is in effect, an exact parallel. Tattoos are very popular at present; I want a specific one to grow on me, the details of which I want entered into my genome and passed on throughout all my generations. I know it will take millions of years, so I think very hard and positive about it. Unfortunately, came the day of my death, and when I died, my notion died with me. Development throughout succeeding generations is a fairy story propagated to bolster a fragile theory.

I like many others, in the belief that evolution was a proven fact, have tried to reconcile my Christian faith with its dogma; and yes, vegetation was the first of all living things to grace our planet, and yes, in the beginning the Earth was without form and void, but other than that, there are no other such comings together. Could it be that God created all things in a form that required an evolutionary process to complete it? That is not the way Genesis tells of the method God used in His creation, and it is cruel to say the least.

In accepting that as a reconciliatory belief, you are saying to God exactly the same as Adam and Eve said, "I don't believe you God, I prefer the account of these others." Be careful, as Scriptures tell us, *a double minded man is unstable in all his ways.* (James 1:8) More importantly, you are saying to God, that He is not telling the truth, it is impossible to believe in a creative God, and believe also in evolution, the two concepts are a universe apart.

Before leaving this section, I want to pass on to you a thought to muse upon throughout your day, reminding ourselves first that man, as we now are, was the last being to populate the planet. It concerns our intelligence and our creativity, just a few thoughts, then over to you.

If we are just another species, think of our achievements in so short a time. Men on the moon, satellite communications, aircraft technology, complex engineering advancements, medical breakthroughs, and so much, much more. Consideration of such things alone tells us emphatically that we are not just another species.

CHAPTER TWELVE
A very Desirable Inheritance

There is no convincing evidence in unfulfilled prophesy. Irrespective of this, I want to share with you some Scriptures that offer us a preview of the eternity that has been prepared for those that put their faith In God. It is no pie in the sky, bye and bye when I die. Having looked at some of the forecasts of God that have been fulfilled, some in the lifetime of many today, why should these that we are going to consider, now fail? Freddy Mercury sang with his group, Queen, *Who wants to live forever?* If the eternal life he envisaged was as this life with all its problems and griefs, but without end, I for one, would be singing alongside him, but it is not . We in this life are living under the curse of Adam, and Jesus dealt with that at Calvary, the new eternal life will be completely different.

So let us preview the life God has promised for those that love him: In order to allow for freedom of flow, I have listed the scriptures used at the end of this section.

We shall no longer have the body of flesh we have now: it will be a spiritual body. *Dear friends now we are children of God, and what we will be has not yet been made known. but we know that when He appears, we shall be like Him; for we shall see him as he is". "it is sown (buried) a natural body: it is raised a spiritual body, if there is a natural body, there is also a spiritual body.*

Marriage and the need to reproduce is no longer relevant. Jesus, when answering the Sadducees on the question of marriage in the next life, gave them this answer, *the people of this age marry, and are given in* marriage; but those who are considered worthy of taking part in that age and in the resurrection from the dead, will neither marry nor be given in marriage, and they can no longer die; for they are like the angels. They are Gods children, since they are the children of the resurrection.

In the book of Revelation, there is a beautiful word-picture of a celebration taking place in heaven; when one of the elders asked the question, *These in white robes, who are they and where did they come from? I answered, "Sir you know" and he said "these are they who have come out of the great tribulation; they have washed their robes and made them white in the blood of the lamb, therefore they are before the throne of God, and serve him day and night in his temple: and he who sits on the throne will spread his tent over them. Never again will they hunger, never again will they thirst. The sun will not beat upon them, nor any scorching heat, for the lamb at the center of the throne will be their shepherd; he will lead them to streams of living Water, and God will wipe away every tear from their eyes.*

Though the language is alien to our modern minds, and may be mentally difficult to envisage, these people, we are told, *are a great multitude which no man could count, from every nation, tribe, people, and language, standing before the throne and in front of the lamb.* Every individual that puts their faith in Christ, now beginning their eternal life in heaven.

Jesus had an unfathomable concern for His disciples, as He has for all of us, and knowing that He was soon to be taken from them, He spends time comforting them. He tells them this: *do not let not your heart be troubled. Trust in God, trust also in me. in my Father's house are many rooms; if it were not so, I would have told you. I am going there to prepare a place for you, and if I go and prepare a place for you, I will come back and take you to be with me that you also may be where I am.*

It is a wonderful thing to know that those words were not for the disciples alone, but for everyone that ever knew Him or knows Him. After His resurrection, Jesus appeared many times as recorded in Scripture, and on two of these occasions more is revealed to us about our expected spiritual life. Twice He came into a locked room and on one visit, He took some boiled fish and honeycomb and ate them. We read that *in a flash, in the twinkling of an eye, we shall be raised from the dead, imperishable, and we shall be changed; we shall have put on the imperishable and the mortal, with immortality.*

And finally a Scripture that really stirs the imagination. *However, as it is written: no eye has seen; no ear has heard, no mind has conceived what God has prepared for those who love him.*

Is it sensible to cast away so great an inheritance, for an improbable theory?

Scriptures used
1, 1 John 3:2, beloved now are we the sons of God.
2, Luke 20:34, there is no marriage in heaven.
3, Revelation 7:13-17, who are these in white robes?
4, Revelation 7:9, before the throne, too many to count.
5, John 14:1-3, do not let your hearts be troubled.
6, John 20:19, Jesus appeared in a locked room.
7, Luke 24:41-43, Jesus ate some food.
8, 1 Corinthians 15:52-54, listen I tell you a mystery.
9, 1 Corinthians 2:9-11, eye has not seen.
10, John 14, 15 and 16, Jesus comforts and reassures his disciples, and us,

CONCLUSION

I have looked closely at some Bible prophesies that have unfailingly proved to be 100% accurate, and have considered our Earth as being a habitat specifically designed for its inhabitants. I also recognised that all things in some way are inter-dependent and we meddle with it to our detriment.

We looked into those ancient prophesies fulfilled in the lifetimes of many of us, as with the Jewish peoples again inhabiting the land of their forefathers. We considered the amazing intricate design in all created things made visible to our generation through advanced technical instruments. We looked at the vastness of the known universe, set against the infinitesimal virtually microscopic planet we all live out our lives on.

We considered the uniqueness of our Earth compared to the inhospitable nature of every other subject of our cosmic investigations, we asked the question, in the light of its distinction, was it designed for a purpose? I offered up an answer in the ultimate crucible section. We considered the flood of Noah, and the geological changes that would be evidenced by it.

I included the testimony of Carol and myself, fifty two days, to illustrate two things. One that spiritual activity is a reality, and two, that when God is invited into a life, things change for the better.

We have throughout, questioned the validity of evolutionary theory and its tenuous credibility in various ways including the absolute necessity for an instant optimum design in creation. Indeed, these writings were instigated to recognise and consider the weakness of evolutions doctrine when set against the unquestionable reliability of biblical prophecy.

For too long now, this pseudo-scientific culture has permeated every avenue of our lives, and time is overdue for a fresh appraisal of its claims.

For since the creation of the world, God's invisible qualities-his eternal power and divine nature- have been clearly seen, being understood from what has been made, so that men are without excuse. (Romans 1:20)

www.ingramcontent.com/pod-product-compliance
Lightning Source LLC
Chambersburg PA
CBHW050506120526
44588CB00044B/1561